Traditional Basque Cooking

THE BASQUE SERIES

English-Basque Dictionary
by Gorka Aulestia and Linda White

Negotiating with ETA:
Obstacles to Peace in the Basque Country, 1975–1988
by Robert P. Clark

Escape via Berlin: Eluding Franco in Hitler's Europe
by José Antonio de Aguirre
introduction by Robert P. Clark

A Rebellious People: Basques, Protests, and Politics
by Cyrus Ernesto Zirakzadeh

A View from the Witch's Cave:
Folktales of the Pyrenees
edited by Luis de Barandiarán Irizar

Child of the Holy Ghost
by Robert Laxalt

Basque-English, English-Basque Dictionary
by Gorka Aulestia and Linda White

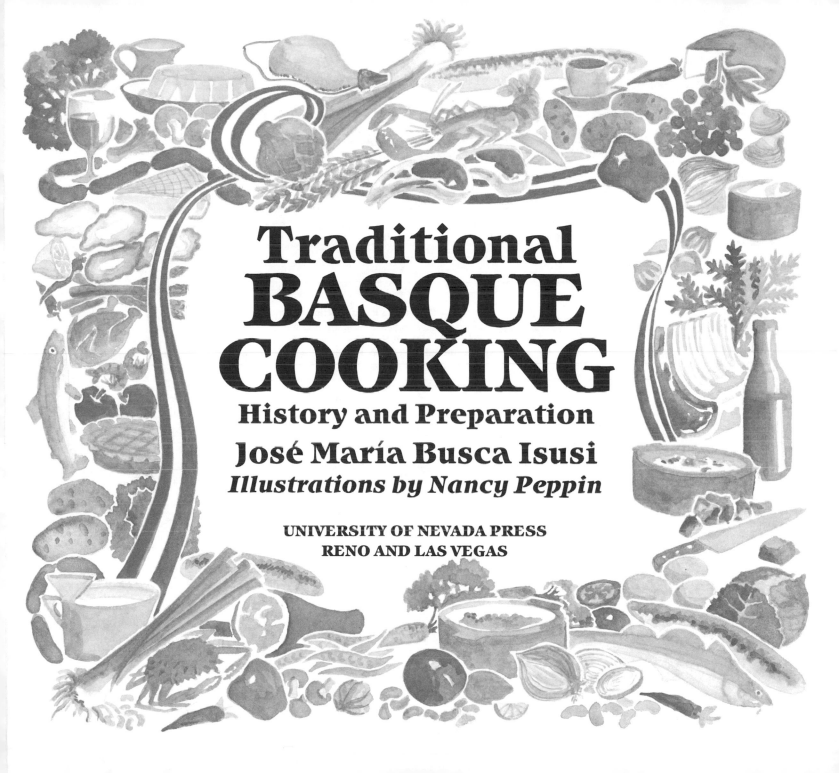

Traditional
BASQUE
COOKING
History and Preparation
José María Busca Isusi
Illustrations by Nancy Peppin

UNIVERSITY OF NEVADA PRESS
RENO AND LAS VEGAS

Originally published as *Alimentos y guisos en la cocina vasca*, by
Editorial Txertoa, © José María Busca Isusi 1983
Translated from the Spanish by Gretchen Holbert

The paper used in this book meets the requirements of American
National Standard for Information Sciences—Permanence of Paper for Printed Library
Materials, ANSI Z39.48-1984. Binding materials were chosen
for strength and durability.

Library of Congress Cataloging in Publication Data

Busca Isusi, José María.
Traditional Basque cooking.
(The Basque series)
Translation of: Alimentos y guisos en la cocina
vasca.
Bibliography: p.
Includes index.
1. Cookery, Basque.   2. Pays Basque (France)—
Social life and customs.   3. Pais Vasco (Spain)—
Social life and customs.   I. Title.   II. Series.
TX723.5.B3B8713   1987   641.6'92'09466   87-10741
ISBN 0-87417-104-0 (alk. paper)
ISBN 0-87417-202-0 (pbk: alk. paper)

University of Nevada Press, Reno, Nevada 89557 USA
© José María Busca Isusi 1987. All rights reserved
Design by Dave Comstock
Printed in the United States of America
1 3 5 7 9 8 6 4 2

Contents

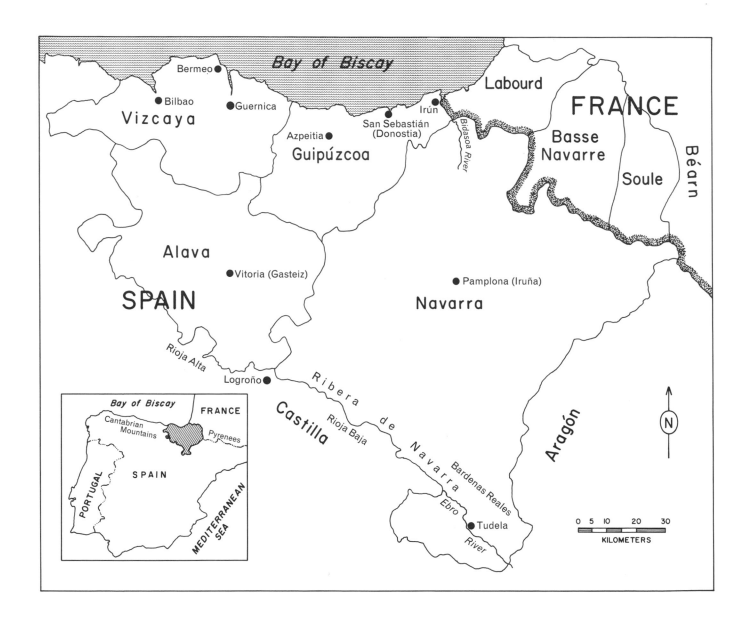

Editor's Preface

THE Basque Country is crossed by two mountain ranges—the Pyrenees on the northeast and the Cantabrian Mountains on the northwest. The humid Cantabrian coastal districts border on the Bay of Biscay. To the south of the main ridges is the semiarid region of central and southern Navarra and Alava. It is to this latter area that the author refers when using the phrase "Mediterranean," since its drainage goes to the Ebro River and eventually to the Mediterranean Sea.

This English translation of the original Spanish edition is altered in its organization to some extent. The five major sections and some smaller portions of text have been rearranged in order to provide a smoother sequence for the reader. Some recipes that appeared in the general text have been moved to the recipe section at the end of the book.

The fourth section on seafood has been slightly changed internally. The original Spanish text used scientific family names for the various groups of mollusks, crustaceans, and fish; this edition uses common English names for the readers' convenience. Scientific names for individual species have been brought up to date and retained in order to avoid the confusion that can occur when only common names are used. People in different geographical regions often use the same common name for different species or different common names for the same species.

Prologue

WHEN one decides to publish his first book, he feels a chill up his spine similar to the one often experienced at decisive turning points throughout life.

It is said that the publication of a book completes one's personality. Having children, planting trees, and publishing books are reputedly the works to be realized by the person of integrated character.

My own personality would have remained largely incomplete if a good friend, Don Fausto Arocena, had not inspired me to write this book [the original Spanish edition] and if he had not at the same time offered to be my pilot in the confusing sea of binding, typography, and galley proofs.

Although the cause is unknown, the fact remains that the theme of human nutrition, particularly as it departs from strictly scientific boundaries, is considered by many to be unworthy of the regard of an educated person.

Without a doubt, the gustatory sense has suffered from bad press. Whereas the pleasurable sensations of hearing, sight, touch, and smell have had poets dedicate the highest degree of inspiration to them, the compositions related to taste are scantier and almost always inspired by a sense of feast and festival.

Perhaps the resentment humanity holds for its own fall hangs over the sense of taste. It was neither the aural nor the olfactory senses, nor riches, nor sexuality that caused the fall of our first parents. It was rather the devouring of an apple that precipitated the loss of grace.

One of the most quoted of biblical adages is that which dictates, "Man does not live by bread alone." This phrase implicitly recognized man's urgent need of bread. In our most exalted prayer we ask for our daily bread without requesting any other material good.

In the Bible, some miracles of Jesus are related to nutrition; one is known as "The Wedding Feast of Cana" in which he changed water into an excellent wine, and another is the miracle of the multiplication of the loaves of bread and the fish.

In the preparation of the Last Supper, the religious and gastronomic rites of Mosaic law were strictly observed, as prescribed for Passover, and today we may reconstruct, to the smallest detail, the development of that supper. In all Mediterranean countries, foods as common as water, wine, bread, and oil play an irreplaceable role in the administration of various religious sacraments.

As regards Basque cuisine, I would say that it embraces much more than is commonly supposed. Basque cooking is more than a simple repertory of culinary recipes prepared for better or worse.

The Basque region, anchored in the valleys and mountains of the Pyrenees since prehistoric times, contains an infinity of data yet to be discovered by anyone who wishes to know something about the origins of Europe itself. Those who concern themselves with the preparation of food in prehistoric times, the vestiges of which are to be found in our Basque kitchens, are in the realm of things little understood.

My goal in writing this book is not one of undertaking a study of ancient food habits nor is it that of producing a definitive work on the subject. I simply propose to deal with the manner by which our culture has resolved the problem of its alimentation through the centuries, in all but a few areas based upon an economy quite limited in regard to alimentary resources. We will finally see, through the culinary methods practiced today, what has resulted from this struggle.

Our culture, without a doubt, has demonstrated great individuality in food preparation; without arriving at the plenitude of French cuisine, there is sufficient quality and originality in our cooking to warrant speaking of a "Basque cuisine." This is a fact recognized by the general public, given that the announcement of Basque cuisine is seen in many culinary establishments—Spanish, French, and Latin American alike. In publishing this book, the effort to produce a digest of Basque dishes has entered into my calculations.

We are in the midst of an epoch of revision, an egalitarian epoch for nations and individuals. The efficiency of communications, the preservation of foods, new agricultural methods, and all of the vertiginous change of the last hundred years are altering our nutrition and our way of life in a manner more radical than that of any other age.

Foods and their means of preparation transcend borders. For many years, we have consumed the garbanzos of Mexico, the meat and milk of the United States, the oils and fats of all the meridians and parallels, the eggs of European and African countries, etc. In our farmhouses a much more varied diet of largely industrialized products is replacing the traditional fare that has existed since almost prehistoric times.

It seems as if we are playing at being sorcerers' apprentices in this synthesis of manufactured and processed foods. With scanty experimentation, products that seem to be innocuous in the short range are thrust upon the general public without the knowledge of possible repercussions for our descendants. Such abundance and uniformity in nutrition could conspire against the human species.

We are in a vortex from which we cannot escape. But in a moving and changing world, we will remain as faithful as possible to our traditional dishes. As Julio Camba says, it could be that we are the last generation to boast of having eaten in a healthy and decent fashion. Already a dawn is foreseen with its horizon full of synthetic products, artificial flavorings, etc.

As a warning to the reader about the content of this book, I would say that it is not just another cookbook. There are excellent ones available and this could never surpass them. The first part of this work is concerned with our alimentary history. Following that, I will discuss the various vegetable and animal species that figure or have figured in the nutrition of the Basques.

When we come upon a particular animal or vegetable species that has a special method of preparation among the Basques, I will explain the steps of the recipe in general terms. More than one reader will say at the end that a typical dish of a village or region has not appeared. If such a thing occurs, I regret the omission.

The task yet remains of completing the consummate work on Basque cooking, and we all must contribute materials to facilitate the eventual completion of that work. The curious reader, anxious to learn more about the field, will find a bibliography at the end of this book.

José María Busca Isusi

I

BASQUE NUTRITION THROUGH THE AGES

THE topic of nutrition in the Basque Country has been little studied. At a conference given by the author in San Sebastián, in January 1951, this neglect was regretted and the theory put forth that the silence imposed by our ethnographers has been fitting, considering the disgrace that we Basques carry of being a gluttonous people.

A few months after this conference I had the great pleasure of meeting Don José Miguel de Barandiarán, the original patriarch of Basque ethnography. He told me that the subject had not been forgotten or evaded.

The matter of nutrition in our culture was in the program of studies of "Eusko-Folkore." Due to various circumstances I do not at this time have complete documentation of the topic. Given that the publication of books on Basque traditions has fortunately resumed, it is hoped that before long we will have a comprehensive work about our nutrition.

I have referred to the gluttonous reputation Basques have among neighboring countries. The Basque people, throughout their history, have known more hunger than satiety. As long as food was abundant, it was consumed in excess, as much to make up for past scarcity as to stock up for the future.

Our ancient code of laws, the *fueros,* does provide rules to prevent the economic catastrophes staged in the Basque Country when weddings, funerals, First Communions, etc., were occasions for overeating. Nevertheless, it is often said that we Basques think about nothing but feasting and gambling. This attitude is similar to the tendency to think of Italians as eternally singing, the French as being in a daily vaudeville, and the Andalucians as always having switchblades.

Iribarren, in his expressive and beautiful books about Navarrese culture and customs, describes the incredible gastronomical feats of Navarrese gluttons. To attribute these deeds to all Navarrese would be excessive.

What occurs is that visitors tend to focus on that which is foreign to them. For this reason, here in the Basque Country where gluttony has dominated us more than lust, the abundance of restaurants and taverns and the lack of dancing places and cabarets are features that draw special attention.

For better understanding of the feast or famine attitude, one should imagine the Basque Country stripped of its modern industrial, commercial, and tourist wealth. Except for the southern region where wheat, wine, and olive oil are produced with facility, the Basque Country offers little in the way of garden produce or other foods.

The two great Basque epic ventures, cod fishing in the Nordic seas and the colonization of extensive zones of the Americas, were motivated by the dire necessity of finding food and also an outlet for overpopulation. The fishing industry, however, affected only a narrow coastal strip of land.

Significant industrial and financial expansion by the Basques in the last seventy-five years has made possible the miracle of being able to maintain a relatively high standard of life, even in the poorest of areas.

In the universal conflict found in all countries between indigenous and exotic customs, those which prove to be incompatible with current modes of living soon disappear. The elaborate regional costumes, the monotonous and incomplete dishes, and the agricultural implements inadequate for modern cultivation all disappear; in short, everything which makes adaptation difficult fades into disuse.

We see, however, that although many things have relinquished territory, three have made their mark in the world: Basque handball, the beret, and certain dishes of Basque cuisine. This is not the place to engage in a discussion about whether or not handball and the beret are genuinely Basque. There is no doubt that these owe their diffusion in the world to us. There are handball courts in the Basque style on all five continents, and during the last war millions of soldiers of all nationalities covered their heads with berets. Our cooking, without claiming the universal diffusion of the French, has extended its influence throughout many countries.

PREHISTORY

A widely recognized theory states that the following took precedence among the first human foods:

- Game

- Harvest of natural foods

- Livestock

- Horticultural products

- Agricultural products

Preparation of the foodstuffs followed these methods:

- Uncooked

- Roasted or baked

- Boiled

The keeping of livestock very well may have begun with the capture of a wounded or young beast and the beginning of agriculture with the observation that where the earth was upturned the plants grew more vigorously. Undoubtedly, the first roast that man ate was from an animal killed in a forest fire caused by lightning or a volcanic eruption.

Man learned to cook before the invention of pottery. He boiled liquids in wooden vessels in which were placed stones heated over live coals. This procedure still proves viable for some primitive Stone Age tribes that are living in this modern century. Basque shepherds still employ this method in the preparation—in their *kaikus* (primitive wooden cooking vessels)—of *mamia,* a curdled sheep's milk. This prehistoric method of preparation has a curious particularity; a burned taste in the concoction is inevitable. Nonetheless, now that it is easy to prepare the curd without it, many Basque gourmets continue to demand that burned taste.

In the Baltic region, investigators of prehistoric culture have found authentic dumping grounds, enabling them to investigate those animals that provided nutrition to the people of that era. In these dumps or *kjokenmoddings* are found the remains of deer, reindeer, wild boars, roe deer, wolves, foxes, wild dogs, bears, lynx, martens, porcupines, beavers, seals, cats, herring, eel, all types of mollusks, swans, penguins, wild cocks, etc. It should be noted that no remains of present-day domesticated animals have been found.

Such abundant and varied remains have not been found in the Basque Country. This could be due to a lack of dumps or simply poor luck in locating them. Nonetheless, prehistoric vestiges appear in our present nutritional practices.

Father Barandiarán draws attention to the fact that remains of land snails rarely appear in our finds whereas they are commonly found in those of neighboring countries. It is very probable, the investigator comments, that the helicophobia of Basque peasants has prehistoric origins. Snails are consumed in the Basque Country in urban areas but very rarely in the rural ones. (I am referring to the Cantabrian area only.)

Primitive Cooking Methods

Some of the practices in the animal butchering can also be considered vestiges of prehistoric procedures.

There are actually primitive people now in Australia that bleed and immediately consume the blood of their prey when hunting the kangaroo. Afterward, the animal is placed in a large oven. The heat causes the expansion of gases in the natural cavities and the bursting of the stomach. The beast is then consumed.

In a Basque hamlet, the killing of a pig resembles a true hunt. The animal is caught with an iron hook in the lower jaw. Once hooked, it is dragged to a table where it is strangled. The task of securing the hog is never achieved by ropes, but rather by the strength of the arms of those present. All the blood is carefully collected by a woman. This blood is not drunk but immediately prepared for the making of blood sausages. These and the liver are the first things to be consumed.

After having been bled, the pig is placed among dry ferns. The ferns are then lit; the fire removes the hair and aids in butchering.

The practice of burning the beast, as outlined above, is carried out in home butcherings, but not in commercial ones. It is now only a tradition, given that today the hogs are nearly smooth and it is unnecessary to depilate them by burning. It is said that this singeing is advantageous to curing and improves the quality of the bacon and ham.

The primitive form of roasting beneath hot coals is still practiced by Basques. Eggs, chorizos, apples and, up until recently in some places, bread have been cooked in this way.

The blood of beef cattle, as well as that of pigs, is consumed together with the intestines. There will be more about this in the section on meat.

From fully grown animals, special sausages called *buzkantzak* or *mondejus* are prepared. This is an autumn dish, of the season in which the shepherds arrive at the valleys from the mountains. In the high zone of Guipúzcoa—Goierri—each town reserves days in which its consumption is almost obligatory.

In Navarra *tripoches* are prepared. The difference between these and the other sausages is that the mixture is made of the small intestine of the lamb or sheep, and blood is not added. The mixture of cooked tripe, onion, and eggs is stuffed into the large intestine and is cooked without previous soaking. *Tripoches* are usually eaten accompanied by a sauce made of lard, garlic, onion, flour, and paprika.

In Zaldivia similar sausages are also called *mondejus* and are eaten

on festival days celebrated at the beginning of October.

In other cuisines, blood is used in the preparation of certain dishes. It is a vital ingredient in civet of hare, a ragout whose singularity is determined by the use of the blood and liver of the hare.

In the famous recipe Duck *a la ruanesa,* the fowl must be strangled and not beheaded. All the blood of the animal is collected without the loss of a single drop.

Utensils

Another aspect of primitivism in Basque cooking is the use of crude ceramic vessels to make the most famous of preparations. The pottery is very rudimentary. Most typical Basque food is prepared in concave-bottomed dishes of baked clay. These *cazuelas* (casserole dishes) have only the suggestion of a handle. The utensil is so connected to food preparation that the recipes themselves are called *cashuelas* or *cashue-litas,* and it is common to eat the food right from the casserole dish.

The interior of the *cazuela* is typically coated with a glaze that prevents the porous clay from absorbing liquids. Even with this precaution, this kind of pottery eventually soaks up fat which, on becoming rancid, can spoil the preparation. Because they are very inexpensive, however, these dishes can be frequently replaced. New ones may also transmit a strange flavor to prepared food. This can be avoided by boiling water and ash in the dishes before use.

Casseroles with concave bottoms do not work well on modern stoves with their flat surfaces. Only placed over coals atop trivets (*iraun-kakoa* or *krispi*) and balanced by braces (*eltzeburniak*) can they be used to full advantage.

As we have seen, clay is inconvenient in some ways but has the great advantage of slowly transmitting heat without metal conductors.

For meat roasted over coals we use metal spits (*burruntziak*), described in the section on meat. They are used to roast the larger pieces. Whole chickens and quails can also be roasted in this manner.

The grill (*arramarrilla*) is used to roast meat cut up into slices, chunks, or small pieces. Fishermen often use the grill for cooking fish. Among these preparations the *besugo* (sea-bream) and sardine excel.

On every farm there are two iron instruments: the *taloburni,* a rod for roasting, and the *tamboliña* (*tamboril*), a perforated metal cylinder bisected by an axle through the base, in which chestnuts are roasted.

Many beverages are served in clay cups. Also the *bota* or *zato* is still widely used in the Basque Country. It is a small wineskin; when well made, it lends an agreeable taste to the wine.

Every day more modern utensils of forged and smelted iron, aluminum, and porcelain are used, but many of our native recipes only reach their apex when prepared and served in clay vessels.

During the prehistoric shepherding season, the women took on the harvesting of vegetable products that nature freely offered. Later they cultivated some of the species in the proximity of their houses. This practice stabilized the familial economy and gave greater importance and influence to the woman within the domestic sphere.

Today vestiges of this organization can still be seen on our farms. The man busies himself with woodcutting and care of the livestock. He overlaps with the woman in agricultural labors when he intervenes in the production and sale of fowl, pigs, and garden produce. He is not at all involved in the cultivation of flax for linen nor in the preparation of land for the same. In the most strenuous agricultural activity, that of plowing, men and women jointly participate as is often seen in classic prints.

The man of the Basque farm has an aversion to gardening and the consumption of its products. He is not very fond of fruits and vegetables. He would rather nourish himself with meat and cheese, but the scarcity of those foods forces him to eat cabbages and leeks.

This aversion of the true Basque peasant, like that of the farmer of the Cantabrian coast, to vegetables is reflected in their regional cuisines —the method for preparing cabbage, leeks, and potatoes is, in general, deplorable. The Basques of the Ribera de Navarra area, however, cook vegetables in an unsurpassed manner. On the plains of Alava, a dish is prepared with the humble potato that is superior to any recipe found in Vizcaya or Guipúzcoa.

Meat and fish continue to be cooked over coals in the most primitive manner. This method, even in the middle of the twentieth century, is unsurpassed, as much from a gastronomic point of view as from one of health.

The roast is a dish that to my understanding enters into the masculine sphere; it belongs to fishermen, hunters, and shepherds. At present, the gastronomic societies of predominantly male membership are the ones in which the preparation of meats is best known, given that the feminine presence is often not well received. Women prefer to stew and bake rather than roast or grill. The persistence of recipes for roasted meats in largely masculine cooking is noteworthy.

THE ANCIENT AGE

Entering the period for which we have written references, we come upon a quote found in the fascinating book by Fausto Arocena, *El País Vasco visto desde fuera* (The Basque Country Seen From Outside). The account is by Strabo and states, "The Basques were sober people and

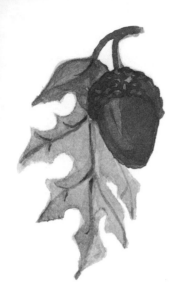

the most common food male goat," and further, "The Basques ate bread made of acorns."

Telesforo de Aranzadi says that the Basques never eat acorns and, quite frankly, I have never seen any of my countrymen enjoying himself eating this fruit. I still recall how surprising it was on my first trip as a student to Madrid to see people eating acorns in the bright autumn days of October. It is certainly true that those particular oak acorns have a sweet taste very different from the bitter and astringent taste of acorns in the Basque Country.

It is possible that the oak was more abundant in ages prior to the present. The fact that the holm oak is widely used in early art could be a confirmation of that theory. Thus, it is quite possible that the Basques in the time of Strabo ate acorns from the holm oak and that upon the disappearance of this particular tree, consumption of the acorn declined.

In those times, in clear contrast to the present, it seems that the Basques did not distinguish themselves by their fondness for strong alcoholic beverages. Beer must have been the most popular drink.

Arocena notes that perhaps Strabo, whose information was hearsay, could have had deficient or altered facts—a problem that even today with all the means of information is a common occurrence—and that beer was in fact a staple, together with cider, male goat meat, and mutton.

Food was prepared with unrendered lard. Our Basque ancestors did not give us a single special dish using male goat; but they did leave behind the most fantastic depictions of the witches' sabbath that the world has ever known which employ the goat as a primary symbol. The pure and original Basque word *akelarre*, meaning witches' sabbath or land of the male goat, has been known and used throughout the world.

Chestnuts were eaten in abundance during this ancient age. The chestnut had been, up until the appearance of corn, the standard fare of our farms throughout the hard winter months. Its harvest is simple; the chestnut does not require much processing. The fruit keeps well for a considerable period of time and when boiled or roasted forms a pleasant-tasting food.

It is a food rich in carbohydrates, although poor in nitrates, and accompanied by milk comprises a very complete meal. It is probable, however, that chestnuts consumed week after week as obligatory fare were gradually regarded as tiresome and monotonous food.

The chestnut, then, had great importance until recently, but the potato has indubitable culinary advantages. In addition to keeping longer than the nut, the potato has more varied uses; it accompanies milk, fish, meat, or eggs and by itself is excellent fried, baked, or boiled.

One arrives at the conclusion that the plague of the honeycomb moth that attacked our chestnut trees constituted a kind of mercy killing. The increasing indifference of the peasant to its fruit and wood, and the preference for the potato and the pine, would have provoked the unmerciful felling of our chestnut forests to clear the land. Today the chestnut is limited to use as a sweet or dessert food, and the farmer generally fells only the dead trees.

THE MIDDLE AGES

On entering our Middle Ages we encounter the inevitable Aymeric Picaud. We don't know what the Basques were like at this point in history, nor what kind of man Picaud was, but the fact remains that this pilgrim of Poitou mounted a strong campaign against our group. As regards nutrition, he called us drunks and said that we ate like pigs or dogs. The democratic customs observed between master and servant seemed detestable to that refined traveler, in the same way that the custom of eating with one's hands did. But as Arocena says, how did man eat in other lands before the invention of the fork?

From other testimonies of this epoch one arrives at the conclusion that the Basque Country was sorely lacking in food resources. For example, the Code of Guipúzcoa prohibited the exportation of cereals and stimulated their importation.

Cider must have been very abundant and wine scarce. Millet flour was used in the preparation of unleavened cakes called *tortas* or *talos*. Wheat had always been scarce due to the lack and poor quality of available land.

In the great poem by Pío Baroja, *La Leyenda de Jaun de Alzate* (The Legend of Jaun de Alzate), the famed Basque novelist intentionally includes an anachronism by representing the Basques as eating corn at the time of Christianization. "I do not want to envision my ancestors eating millet," says Don Pío, "as if they were a flock of goldfinch."

It was during the Middle Ages that the Basques initiated their codfishing enterprises in the northern seas in competition with the Nordic peoples. The struggle must have been considerable, the difficulties enormous. One only has to think about how, with small ships, they could have sailed in the most formidable tempests known—those off the coasts of Newfoundland!

There are no other people who venerate codfish (*bacalao*) as the Basques do. To other nations codfish is a necessary evil. They consume it when they have nothing else. But here it is prepared with great care and its presence is always welcomed in any season and on any table.

This love of codfish is probably due to the memory of its difficult and painful capture and is a gesture of gratefulness for its role in preventing hunger among our people through the centuries.

It was in the Middle Ages that Basques possessed the fame of being

great whale fishermen. However, these mammals have been unable to bear centuries of continued capture and have been greatly reduced in number.

I am convinced that our fishermen, so adept in their culinary preparations, would have had some magnificent recipes for the preparation of whale meat and intestines. I have not been able to find any recipe that could be called "Whale Basque Style," but I am certain that such a formula existed in some time period.

The original code of laws from Guipúzcoa reveals that dried conger eel was a common dish during the Middle Ages. Today, the conger eel can still be found off of our coasts but not in sufficient quantity to be regarded as a popular food.

Finally, regarding the Middle Ages in the Basque Country, I once again quote from Arocena's book, though somewhat reluctantly. The ancient baron of Rosmithal says about a country then called Biskein:

> In this country there is no need of a horse; there is no hay, no straw, there are no stables and furthermore, the lodgings for travelers are poor. The wine is kept in goatskins. One cannot find good bread, meat, or fish; for the most part, the people live on fruit.

THE MODERN AGE

The discovery of America had two immediate repercussions of deep significance to the Basque Country.

Demographically it provided the opportunity to reduce the congestion of the overpopulated region; furthermore, in many cases, the emigrant made his fortune in America, and that returning foreign capital formed the basis of our present economic progress.

On the nutritional side, the introduction of corn was a fundamental

boost to our agriculture. In truth, we can speak of two periods of agriculture—the time before corn was introduced and the period after its introduction.

Corn

Corn seems to have been introduced by one Gonzalo de Perkaiztegui who could have been related to a bishop, a native of Hernani. Little information exists about this great benefactor, so little that our erudite Dr. Gárate has recommended that I make an investigation into the archives of the Vatican to find a trace of Perkaiztegui.

We have repaid with ingratitude this act by Perkaiztegui, and I believe that today, except on one street in Hernani, his name is virtually unrecognized. It is a shame that the name of this man is unknown by the vast majority of his countrymen—even by those of greater than average culture and education—when we have so many plaques and street names honoring celebrities of little importance.

Corn adapted itself so well to our environment that it has become identified with our land. There is nothing that better depicts the Cantabrian coast than a farmhouse surrounded by a cornfield.

Despite its being foreign, corn soon had a Basque name (*arto*). It soon replaced millet in the native diet. Millet was literally swept from our fields. The sweeping away was fitting, given that the small amount of millet that is cultivated today is used to make the finest brooms.

Corn is a very dependable crop in the Basque Country. Summer grain makes few demands in this humidity; corn resists hailstones, and if it does contract disease, it is never serious enough to ruin the harvest.

Corn can be eaten by man and beast alike. In the form of unleavened bread, or as a pancake and accompanied by milk, it forms the basis of the diet of our laborers. Today, however, it seems as if a decline in human consumption is beginning to occur.

As a nutriment for livestock it is, I think, the best substance for obtaining meat of high quality.

Discretion is recommended in the use of corn as a feed for laying hens. It appears that chickens fed with corn lay fewer eggs, but they are of a unique quality. In no other European country (among the five or six that I am familiar with) have I eaten eggs of quality similar to those produced by our corn-fed chickens.

In the techno-agricultural sense, corn permitted the establishment of an alternative that has proved ideal for three hundred years. The corn-wheat-turnip rotation is still established on many farms. Economically this alternative has failed in the case of wheat and is beginning to fail for corn, due to the fact that its use, as I see it, must endure competition from hybrid corns produced today on large, highly mechanized farms.

Beans

In the field, rows of corn are alternated with rows of red beans. In the shade of the cornstalks, this bean acquires a truly unique, mild flavor. The famous beans of Tolosa are of this type.

During seasons of standard labor, the red bean forms the basis of the laborers' boiled dinner on the Cantabrian coast. The inhabitant of the Basque farm dislikes the white bean, which he denigrates as having little nutritional value.

Until recently, great quantities of dried broad beans were consumed. Very rich in protein, these took the place of meat on the tables of the poor. Men and animals engaged in hard labor were nourished basically by beans. They were boiled with salted lard (*gantz*) and accompanied by the corn pancake.

The cultivation of broad (horse) beans was previously quite exten-

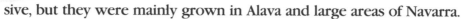

sive, but they were mainly grown in Alava and large areas of Navarra.

The name *babazorros* (horse-bean eaters)—taken from the Basque *baba* or Spanish *haba* and given to the native people of Alava—is a misnomer, considering that the consumption and cultivation of the bean is now greatly decreased. The gap left by beans has been filled by the potato, another American contribution to our agriculture and cuisine.

Potatoes

The introduction of the potato was quite late in the Basque Country. This tuber, popularized by Parmentier, encountered many obstacles in its diffusion. The people resisted eating it, and it was only cultivated as animal fodder.

In Alava, however, the potato found a very favorable milieu for its consumption and cultivation. Soon, beans were largely replaced by potatoes in the field as well as in the kitchen. Something similar occurred in large areas of Navarra such as the Barranca.

Times of shortage usually contribute to the spreading of the consumption of little-appreciated products. This fact has been evidenced among us in relation to the potato. It is cultivated in the Cantabrian zone to a much greater extent than before 1936 (the Spanish Civil War). Enormous consumption of potatoes occurred until 1950, and although clearly declining now, it is still much greater than before 1936.

The current decrease in consumption is due in the first place to a tendency (every day more common) to eat fewer boiled dinners and in the second place to the somewhat unfortunate hybridizations of European geneticists. They have developed potatoes with greater productivity and resistance to disease, but they seem to have forgotten quality. Thus, the present varieties of potatoes are of inferior culinary value when compared with the old varieties. These two reasons may be the causes of the lack of demand that now is threatening potato farmers in areas of Alava and Navarra.

Wheat

I will conclude this historical tour with a mention of wheat. Previously we noted that grains had always been scarce and wheat the scarcest among them all. For many centuries white wheat bread has been a luxury among the Basques. The bread that is consumed today is made with flours from the grain of Navarra, Alava, Castilla, etc., and even from much American and Turkish wheat.

To synthesize that which has been the diet of the Basques, I will summarize what has been said in the often-quoted book of Arocena regarding the impressions of various visitors to our Basque Country.

In 1494 an Armenian bishop, Martiros, called Vizcaya the "land where fish is eaten."

In 1501 Señor de Montigny, of the retinue of Phillip the Handsome, spoke of having partaken of sugary pastries according to the national custom in Fuenterrabía. In Vitoria he saw a knight who was truly adept at butchering.

In 1572, Venturino said of Vizcaya and Guipúzcoa that they were needy and that millet bread and cider were consumed.

In 1610, Dr. Gaspar Stein said that the Cantabrians were devoted to fish, especially those fish called *bacalao* (salt cod).

In 1633, the Franciscan Venerable Bell said that in San Sebastián, "parsley, beer, and English cheese" were eaten. It can be deduced from this that maritime commerce had expanded the diet, at least in the seaports. The same Franciscan said that in the market of San Adrián all that a man would need to eat and drink could be found.

In the year 1700, an English booklet by an anonymous author, *An Account of San Sebastián,* said that the diet of the inhabitants of San Sebastián included chocolate in the morning and at midday, soup stocks of meat in clay casserole dishes, roasted meat, stew, and dessert, all of this complemented by wine. In not mentioning cheaper foods or cider, the author doubtlessly was referring to foods eaten by people of high economic position.

In the same book it said that the apples were good and plentiful, wheat scarce and imported from Denmark, the Barbary Coast, and England, and that in times of shortage, a bread of chestnut flour was concocted. Rabbits from Navarra and pheasants from Aragón were also encountered.

Fish was abundant, even though the decline of cod-fishing sites began at this time. Ships existed that were devoted to whale hunting.

Bowles stated that in 1775 it was rare to see a drunken Basque, an affirmation that would not as easily be made in our own era. The phenomenon was explained not because of natural sobriety, but due to the fact that before beginning to drink, people ate abundantly. It is not clear whether we eat less or drink more at present.

In 1778, Juan Laglancé described the delicacies of the eels in Bilbao and of squid with their "black liquor." He noted that the people of Bilbao of every class were very given to the pleasures of the table.

He also told about a particular feast that was composed of the following: two soups; boiled chicken; five kinds of roasted meats; five plates of pastries and mincemeats; five main dishes or entrees; five secondary courses; and puddings, desserts, fruit, and coffee. All was set off by wines among which those of Bordeaux stood out. Throughout the meal, sweet peppers the size of a little finger were also served.

Humboldt noted in 1801 that the vineyards of Guetaria devoted to *chacolí,* a white Basque wine, had vines supported by whale vertebrae.

In 1817, the Count of Laforest said that tuna was cured in Bilbao with as much delicacy as in Nantes. Today this dish is almost unknown and *mojama* (salted tuna of the Mediterranean coasts) is only served in a few establishments.

The palate of the Frenchman Teófilo Gautier found the flavors of our cuisine acceptable, except for oil and paprika.

Ozanam, one of the most illustrious of gourmets, liked our foods, especially chocolate with *esponjas* (meringue cookies). It is unknown if these cookies could be the delicious ladyfingers—made in so many villages until recently—that are dipped in chocolate, or the *bolaos,* made with sugar syrup and beaten egg white—the authentic hardened *esponja* that is stirred in the inevitable glass of water that accompanies the cup of chocolate.

The wife of Bascophile Van Eys couldn't bear our squid dishes, although she accepted the rest of our food. Like the majority of northern Europeans, she was bothered by garlic.

Although Arocena's book ends with the Dutchwoman's comments, the number of visitors increased after the 1868 visit by the Van Eyses. The first observation of the vast majority of them concerned the smell of garlic and oil not only in the kitchens but also in the streets. It is well established that those who remain some time among us become accustomed to these smells.

It is a universal fact that every group of people prepares its basic dishes in an unequaled manner. Accordingly, we have the excellent Galician pottages or *potes;* the Asturian bean stews or *fabadas* of pork and beans; Valencian *paellas* or rice casseroles; Andalucian *gazpacho* or cold vegetable soup; *eltzekaria,* a stew made by the French Basques on the other side of the Bidasoa River; our Basque *cocidos* or boiled dinners, and our *marmitakos* or tuna stews. All these recipes are cooked in an unsurpassable way, even in the humblest of kitchens.

Today in the preparation of foods, as in all human activities, Basques are in the middle of an evolutionary period. The various sources of energy applied to food preparation, the lack of domestic help, the new hygienic rules for food promulgated by physicians, the great expansion of preserved and precooked foods, etc., are eliminating the old formulas from our kitchens.

But the present tendency toward simpler preparation must not cause the ancient recipes to be forgotten. On the contrary, since they are not standard fare, they will become even more highly regarded as delicacies.

This urge to preserve the past is not motivated only by egoism. We have the obligation to transmit these old recipes to our descendants. Furthermore, every day tourism increases in our country, giving us an opportunity for economic growth and cultural communication. The obligatory consumption of food by tourists brings forth our greatest propaganda— if the foods are prepared according to authentic recipes.

To each visitor we must present a selection of dishes in sufficient quantity and specialization so that all who come here, upon returning home, will speak of the existence of a Basque cuisine.

2

VEGETABLES

IN the territory geographically and historically known as the Basque Country, there exists a great diversity of climate and terrain that makes possible an extremely varied vegetable production.

The southern region is anchored in the land of the olive tree and the grapevine; the high Pyrenean area is clearly one of pines; and along the coasts in a mild and humid climate, orange and lemon trees are cultivated.

There are also semiarid zones (for example, the Bardenas Reales), saline grounds, swamps, and forests occupied by a great variety of plant species, untilled land, fern fields, and gorse thickets.

With such a diverse climatology and a no less varied geological makeup, our land has been able to provide all types of agricultural products, with the exception of those of a subtropical or tropical nature. However, the variety and quality of vegetables has not presupposed abundance nor an adequate distribution of such produce.

Until the middle of the nineteenth century with the opening of the railroads, Navarrese wine reached the coastal towns with great difficulty. The lack of wine in these towns necessitated the cultivation of vineyards in places where production was poor and insufficient. The popular drink was cider. The same problem of transportation and supply held true for wheat from Navarra, and shipment of wheat was made by sea from other countries.

Today it is easy to provide for our nutrition not only with indigenous vegetable products but also with those from distant regions.

Our region presents limited possibilities for the cultivation of the olive tree, the grapevine, the pepper, the peach tree, etc. Within these limits, however, products are frequently of the highest quality. It seems as if in zones where climate benignly permits cultivation, plants develop the best culinary characteristics.

The temperate zone is that which produces the best plants for human nourishment. The tropics, with all their exuberance, do not offer vegetables that compete with those of the temperate regions, although they do provide products that grow only in a tropical environment.

The quality of the produce is affected not only by climate but also by the nature of the soil and the activity of man. Procedures of cultivation, genetic applications, and developmental techniques are decisive factors in the quality of the harvests. In spite of the fact that we have vegetable products of high quality, we see a clear possibility of improvement.

The aspect which is most ignored is that of presentation. It is to be hoped that in the coming years we will succeed in presenting produce which, without losing its culinary qualities, has an appearance similar to foreign fruits and vegetables that surpass ours in this aspect (although they are not as flavorful).

Let us review the different plants that enter into Basque nutrition. In general, I will use the Basque or Spanish common names. The scientific name will be applied only when the popular name does not designate exactly the species to which I refer.

MUSHROOMS

Mushrooms grow in abundance in the Basque Country, and it seems as if they have been consumed since earliest times. They grow mainly in forests, untilled lands, fern fields, and pastures.

There exist numerous poisonous species, and there is a need for caution to be exercised. Poisoning by mushrooms occurs because of inexperience or overeagerness on the part of the gatherer. One must discard all mushrooms that seem at all suspicious. The species that I will mention, however, are easy to recognize, even with limited experience.

For the sake of prevention, excellent mushrooms are left needlessly unconsumed. In Guipúzcoa the *lamperna* (parasol mushroom, *Lepiota procera*) is hardly eaten, whereas it is doubtlessly valued in Alava. On the other hand, the *urrechas* and *gibelurdinak,* excellent mushrooms of the genus *Russula,* are not eaten in many towns of Alava yet are highly esteemed in Guipúzcoa.

A Basque of the Ribera region would be aghast at seeing a farmer eat

---

Editor's note: This section should be read for interest and methods of preparation but not for guidance in mushroom selection. Because of the differences existing between European mushrooms and their seeming counterparts in North America (and because of the similar appearance of poisonous and nonpoisonous species), extreme caution is advised. All wild varieties should be checked by an expert. It should also be noted that mushrooms do not affect all individuals in the same way.

the multicolored mushrooms that grow between ferns and beech trees, whereas the farmer would not even try the mushrooms associated with the black poplar that are found in the *calderillos* (small hollows) of the Ribera.

In that this work has no botanical pretensions, I will set aside those poisonous and otherwise suspicious species and maintain that on our tables we do find examples of healthy, young, and newly gathered mushrooms.

For the reader who wishes to study the differentiation among the species, I have cited at the end two books by authors of the Basque Country concerning this matter.

Tricholoma (*Calocybe*)

The mushrooms of San Jorge—*zizak,* also called *perretxikoak* in Alava—belong to the genus *Tricholoma* (more recently classified as species of *Calocybe*). The three species involved are closely related, and *T. georgii* and *T. albellum* are probably varieties of *Calocybe gambosum,* the St. George's mushroom. They appear in the spring, are of yellowish-white color and of small to medium size, and are extraordinarily aromatic. They are gathered in many areas, but those of Alava and Orduña are the most famous.

To the Alavese, they are almost a totem, and the feast of the patron saint Prudencio de Armentia must necessarily be celebrated with a meal which includes these *perretxikoak.* Although they may be prepared in many ways, they are best in an omelet.

Amanita, Russula, Boletus, Psalliota, Cantharellus

Among the *Amanita, Russula, Boletus, Psalliota,* and *Cantharellus* genera are found the most common of mushrooms, many of which are poisonous.

Within the group *Amanita* we have the magnificent *Amanita caesarea* (*oronja, kuleto,* or *amboto*), a large, beautiful orange mushroom that appears at the end of summer. It is excellent prepared in an omelet or fried, but its magnificence is fully realized when it is grilled over coals with a little oil, garlic, and parsley.

In the genus *Russula,* we use three species: *R. virescens* (*Rúsula de Cura, gibelurdin,* or *shanjuan*); R. cyanoxantha (*urrecha* or *gibelurdin*); and *R. heterophylla* (also called *gibelurdin*), probably a variety of *R. cyanoxantha.* All three types are excellent in an omelet or baked in the oven. An explanation must be made concerning the common names of these mushrooms. The name *gibelurdin,* clearly Basque, is a word admitted by the Spanish Academy (as *guibelurdiñ*) even though there are Spanish words to designate it.

The genus *Boletus* has two edible varieties: *B. edulis* (the pumpkin mushroom, *onto-zuriya*), and *B. aereus* (blackhead, *onto-beltz*). Both are excellent and of fine meat, even though they become a little sticky when cooked.

Within the genus *Psalliota* (now called *Agaricus*) we find *P. campestris* (the meadow mushroom, *azpibeltza*), an excellent mushroom little appreciated in the Basque Country when wild, but highly valued when cultivated. The popular *champignon* of our bars and kitchens is nothing more than the cultivated *azpibeltza,* yet here occurs one of the paradoxical preferences of public taste. The excellent wild mushroom, abundant and easy to gather, is superseded by the domesticated version, which is of lesser quality and very expensive. The *azpibeltza* is the only mushroom that has been submitted to domestication.

The most common of mushrooms are without a doubt those of the genus *Cantharellus*. Its best-known species is *C. cibarius* (*cabrilla, salsa-perretxiko*), which grows abundantly in our forests. It is a mushroom of leathery meat and little scent, but as it is easily dried, it is usually gathered with the express purpose of saving it for winter.

Other Varieties

Many other mushrooms exist which, although excellent, are not well known. They are eaten in specific regions, and almost none of the following varieties have a Basque name: the *morillas* or morels of the genus *Morchella*; the rat's foot or fairy club mushrooms in the genus *Clavaria*; the *gamuza* of the genus *Hydnum*; the *negrilla* in the genus *Tricholoma*, near relatives of the *zizak*; the *plateras* of *Clitocybe*; and the nonpoisonous *níscalos* of the genus *Lactarius*, highly appreciated in Cataluña and left unappreciated by Basques. Every year *níscalos* are exported to Cataluña from the valleys of northern Navarra at the cost of some hundreds of thousands of pesetas.

Final Considerations

In our country it is uncommon to prepare these mushrooms in sauce. *Salsa-perretxikoak* are used as a complement to meat dishes during wintertime, when it is difficult to find other varieties.

The spring dish of the *zizak* omelet is usually the most expensive of the season. Incredible prices are paid for the mushrooms. Only the prices of the season's first eels approach a similar level.

The Alavese recipe for an omelet is in the line of two other great Basque omelets: the *piperrada* and the *frikatza*. Of these three great concoctions only the *piperrada* has—without possessing more merit than the others—entered into the repertories of international cuisine.

Truffles are little known or used in the Basque Country. A methodical investigation would probably find places where these magnificent fungi grow.

Criadilla de tierra, a white truffle, is found with relative frequency. It belongs to the genus *Terfezia,* and although its flavor does not equal the delicacy of other truffles, it is nonetheless excellent. In Mallavia, good ones of ample size, cooked like other truffles, do honor to the most elaborate table.

GRAINS

The cultivation of grains marked an enormous advance in human culture, as much from a hygienic point of view as from an economic one. Grains provide proteins and carbohydrates in a form easily digestible by our bodies. They are also excellent food for animals and may be preserved for many months without spoilage. With the cultivation of grain, man regularized his diet and sustained his domestic animals in times when pasturage was scarce.

Grain is eaten upon reaching total maturity and thereby attains its maximum quality and properties of preservation. In some areas corn is eaten before it reaches maturity, but in our country this is of anecdotal interest only.

The milling of grain dates from prehistoric times. Homer said that "the mills of the gods grind slowly, but grind continuously." This phrase is as applicable to the atomic age as it was to the Homeric.

Flour from grain cannot be eaten raw. The abundant starch that it contains would form a paste when mixed with saliva and would make digestion impossible. If the flour is roasted, the starch is dextrinized and caramelized. The Basques have not typically roasted their flours. In the Canary Islands, however, roasted flour (*gofio*) is the favorite dish.

In the past, *gachas* (porridge made from wheat flour dissolved in water or milk) was popular among Basques.

Morokil is corn mush, and *aya* is a mush made of wheat flour. Today these foods are disappearing from our diets. It must be noted, however, that during the famine of the 1940s, *morokil* was eaten a great deal in urban centers. It is an easy dish to make, very complete as regards nutrition, and easily digested if well prepared. At present, *aya* and *morokil* are prepared almost exclusively for children.

Corn

Talo is made with a soft dough of water, salt, and corn flour which is later formed into a patty and cooked over an iron grill called a *talo-burni.* It is a very primitive dish but quite delicious and nutritious, given that it is generally broken up in milk. Sometimes it is substituted for bread during meals. Regardless of the evolution of the diet, *talo* continues to be the basis of nutrition for many of our farmers.

Talo dough is formed by adding tepid water to corn meal until it reaches sufficient consistency to form soft balls. These balls should be about the size of a medium-sized orange. Once formed, they are left to rest next to the fire. Over a smooth, floured table, these balls are flattened into patties with small blows of the hand. A skilled maker can produce circular patties which are very thin and without breaks.

The patties are placed over a hot *taloburni* or grill. During cooking, the granules of the moistened corn meal expand from the action of the heat and form the typical large bubbles. The amount of heat affecting the dough is enormous in comparison to the smallness of the patties; on the other hand, the temperature is very high and consequently the water in the dough evaporates rapidly. The starch dextrinizes and caramelizes and even burns in some places, producing the dark spots that later will add a delicious flavor to the milk.

Good *talo* should consist of only two layers without dough between them. If the balls have been made into thick patties, a doughy and indigestible center is left.

If this center were to be cooked, the patty would have to be placed on a less intense fire for a longer period of time. We would have a very different result than the *talo* previously described.

Also with corn meal, an unleavened bread is made which is called *arto* in Basque and *borona* in Spanish. The dough for this bread is made with less water than that of *talo* and is left to set a longer time. The cooking temperature is lower, given that *arto* is cooked in an oven, not on a sheet of iron placed over the flames.

It is customary to cook the cornbread on a cabbage leaf. The imprints of the leaf veins leave their mark on the bread.

Arto has a thick and doughy appearance and is not very suitable as an accompaniment to other dishes. Therefore, it is usually cut into thin slices and cooked in milk for a long time. In this way it makes a very pleasing and nutritious meal.

The Basques, when engaged in arduous labor, prefer breads made of corn to those of wheat. Ironworkers and coal miners have been great consumers of corn. It seems that this preference is due to economic motives. Wheat bread has a more subtle taste and is more easily digested; those mighty men could have eaten great quantities of wheat bread. However, that action would have thrown their meager budget out of balance. Because of this, they ate cornbread in place of wheat and broad beans in place of the smoother French beans.

Corn flour has substantially more oil than that of other grains and for this reason spoils more quickly. Corn flour must be used quickly after milling, whereas wheat flour can remain for months without spoilage.

The varieties of corn that have traditionally been cultivated produce an excellent flour for human consumption. The farmers who still eat corn do not wish to replace these excellent but low-yielding varieties with the more prolific double hybrids of inferior quality.

Wheat

In the Basque Country wheat has generally been scarce except in the areas of the Mediterranean slope, where it is of very high quality, given that it has a high gluten content. The varieties from the Bardenas Reales region of Navarra are exceptional and together with those of the Cinco Villas Aragonesas are without a doubt the best in all the peninsula. These kinds of wheat are fought over by those dedicated to the confection of cakes and fine pastries in Barcelona, Madrid, Bilbao, and San Sebastián.

The bread eaten in some of the villages situated on the fringes of Bardenas, like Cabanillas or Fustiñana, is unsurpassable.

The bread that was and still is produced in small local bakeries is made with less leavening and water than in the large-scale commercial bakery firms. The flour produced in the small mills along our rivers is less refined than that produced in the factories, but without a doubt its nutritional value is greater.

On the farm, bread is usually formed and baked once a week. The shortage of leavening and water produces a bread that lasts for many days. In the tough economy of the Basque farm, the consumption of tender and spongy bread would be ruinous.

The Basque proverb which Azkue quotes says it quite well:

Eguneko ogia itxe-galgarria
(Daily bread, bad for the house)

Up until a short time ago, there were farms that made bread according to a prehistoric tradition, beneath hot coals. Today this is forgotten and bread is made in simple ovens which are valued just as highly.

Other Grains

Even though it is nothing more than a historical memory, I must make mention of millet, quite popular in the Basque diet until the appearance of corn. Millet is still widely cultivated by primitive peoples of Asia, Africa, and Oceania.

Along the Cantabrian coast, barley, oats, and rye are neither cultivated nor used for human nutrition. In the Mediterranean region, they have some importance, as they are grown for animal fodder. Barley does enter into Basque nutrition through its use in beer.

Rice is being introduced as a crop and as a food in a gradual way. In the southern cultivated lands of the Ebro River, excellent rice is produced, as fine as the best Levantine rice. Climate is the only barrier to the expansion of rice cultivation—it is grown in a limited area, and the lack of sufficient heat has harmed some harvests.

The culinary preparation of rice requires much care and technique due to the mucilaginous substance that it contains. To prevent this substance from acting as an agglutinant and ruining the preparation, two methods are employed.

In one, the amount of water and the cooking time are strictly controlled in order to avoid the occurrence of mucilage. This is the formula that, with a few variations, is provided: twice the quantity of water as that of rice and twenty minutes to cook. In this way the rice is barely cooked when the water is used up. Valencian *paella* is the most popularized dish of this type of preparation.

In the other procedure, the rice is cooked in large quantities of water in such a way that the mucilage becomes very diluted and loses its

agglutinant properties. Indian rice curries are prepared according to this method.

In the Basque Country, and principally on our farms, we find ourselves midway between the two methods, which is not a virtue in this instance. These lines are offered as a piece of advice to the reader who is unfamiliar with the rice *paellas* served in our country homes which consist of gummy mixtures of grains of rice and more or less flavorful pieces of meat and fowl.

In many Basque areas, rice is used as a filling for blood sausage. To my understanding, the rice stuffing has a dual purpose: that of augmenting the volume and of facilitating preservation. Blood sausages stuffed with onion and leek spoil quickly.

In the now classic argument between supporters of blood sausage made with rice and those who support the use of vegetables, I would join the latter camp. Onion and leek have distinctive and unadulterated flavors and are widely used as spices in cooking, whereas rice, with its almost imperceptible taste, can add nothing more to sausage than its physical characteristics.

LEGUMES

Legumes are second in importance to grains in relation to human nutrition. However, these plants are very rich in protein, and in this respect they are superior to grains. The flour from legumes is not appropriate for breadmaking.

Basques eat large quantities of French beans and broad beans (also called horse beans) and small amounts of peas, garbanzos, and blue vetch. In this legume section, I will refer to the mature and dried grain. The green, unripened form will be discussed in the section on garden produce.

Broad Beans

Habas (broad beans) have served, together with *talo* and salted lard, as the basis for the nutrition of those engaged in heavy physical labor. Different varieties of these beans, possessing varying properties of smoothness and size, are cultivated and consumed, and each type has its advocates.

Broad beans constitute a hearty and nutritious dish that in periods of want can act as a meat substitute. Their cultivation is simple. They are planted around All Soul's Day (November 2) and are harvested at the beginning of summer. In many of the Cantabrian areas, wheat and broad beans are planted together in strips. The rows of broad beans function as wind barriers and prevent the wheat from collapsing.

Up until recently, broad bean cultivation was widespread throughout the Basque Country. Now, however, the growing of these beans for seed is limited to a few areas of Alava and Navarra.

Given the present evolution of food tastes and the rising standard of living, it might not be extreme to assume a rapid disappearance of the broad bean as a legume for human consumption. The potato has almost totally replaced the broad bean in the field and in the kitchen.

Red Beans

Today, the truly popular legume among the Basques is a bean called the *alubia*. Many varieties of this bean are edible, but we eat only the red, white, and mottled (pinto) ones. Other kinds are unknown to us.

In the Cantabrian region the red bean, or kidney bean, is the most popular type. It is generally grown in strips together with corn. Perhaps because this bean is raised in highly fertilized, acidic soils and grows in the shade of the corn, it acquires a smoothness after cooking that is not found in other kinds of beans. Cooked kidney beans produce a characteristic chocolate-colored broth.

The popular *cocido* (bean stew) is prepared with this bean; pork fat is used in cooking this dish, but olive oil can also be utilized. Red beans, in any form, are generally eaten at the midday meal.

An observation must be made here in relation to beans. These legumes, so highly appreciated by us, are systematically rejected by domestic and wild animals. Beans have hardly ever been destroyed by insect plagues. Only during years of need were beans imported from various other sources, and then it was attributed to a weevil which infested the stored grain.

Beans are never consumed by birds or rodents in the fields or in the storehouses, even during the hardest of winters. Neither cattle, sheep, nor pigs try them. Only hungry dogs will eat cooked beans.

I haven't been able to find a single reference as to the cause of this aversion, and worse yet, I do not have the slightest idea to what it is due.

White Beans

In many areas of the Mediterranean, white beans—disliked by the Guipuzcoan and Vizcayan farmers—are consumed by preference. The Basque farmers consider them to be of lesser nutritional value and say, "It's the same eating them as carrying them around in one's pockets."

The custom exists of harvesting white beans before they reach full maturity, when the grain is formed but not hardened. The color must be greenish white. The name *pochas* must have come, contrary to general opinion, from their uneven or mottled (*pocho*) color. The other meaning of that word cannot be applied—*pocho* also being that which is overly ripe or rotten. With this white bean a stew of exceptional smooth-

ness is prepared. Two classic recipes from Navarra are *pochas* prepared with quail and *pochas* with eel, both excellent. White beans are frequently eaten accompanied by vegetables, and sometimes by tomatoes.

TUBERS AND ROOTS

Basques have not been very fond of roots and tubers as a nutritional source. The turnip is only used as forage, and the hybrid strains of Cruciferae, so popular in many regions of Europe, are unknown. Beets do not have any other use than as a commercial plant or feed. The colored Egyptian variety is consumed only in a limited way in our urban centers.

Until recently the potato was used only as hog feed. It seems that its consumption became more common among the Basques when, in the middle of the last century, foreign workers arrived for the construction of the railroads. In Alava and Navarra its diffusion was rapid, but much slower in Guipúzcoa, Vizcaya, and areas in the region of the Bidasoa River. The widespread popularization and consumption of the potato actually occurred during the years of scarcity in the 1940s.

The greater popularity of the potato could be due to the significant characteristics that it possesses:

○ Economy. Its cultivation is easy, and even in mediocre soils it provides good harvests.

○ Ease of cooking. It is very easily prepared in a relatively short time. The same facility holds true when it is baked or fried.

○ Culinary versatility. The potato is a perfect accompaniment to vegetables, legumes, eggs, fish, or meat. Alone and with various seasonings, it constitutes an excellent dish.

The quality of our potatoes is in general quite good. In some areas of

Navarra and Alava it is exceptional. The excellence of the product is lower among different varieties in which production yield and resistance to disease are considered before quality. It is hoped that before long we can count on those delicious potatoes, the *bizcocheras,* from the area of Salvatierra.

The potato pottage of the Alavese plain is superb. It is not as well prepared in Guipúzcoa, where the potato is generally overcooked. It seems as if the secret of the Alavese dish, apart from the quality of the potato, is in rapid cooking and in the use of very fresh peppers of top quality.

GARDEN PRODUCE

In general the garden produce of our land is excellent and, on occasion, exceptional. But whatever the quality, it must be eaten freshly picked or at least correctly canned at an adequate temperature.

Once harvested or separated from the main plant, the vegetable's cells are unable to continue their normal functions. Due to the disconnection from the root, the cells consume the assimilable products in their proximity and true autolysis occurs. This process is much more accentuated when the temperature is greater. If the harvest of the product requires causing damage to the plant, as is the case with asparagus, deterioration is usually rapid.

This rapid spoilage impedes the consumption of good-quality asparagus in areas somewhat separated from those of its production. For the majority of people, the impossibility of eating good, fresh asparagus has resulted in their preference for the canned vegetable; although it is excellent, it does not equal the taste of the admirable spring asparagus of the Ribera de Navarra.

Climate, the reaction of the soil, and cultural practices all affect the

quality of vegetable products, with the result that we have a great diversity of garden produce in our land.

Artichokes

Artichokes produced in the Ribera de Navarra region are unsurpassable. They are smaller and tastier than various French varieties. The best artichoke is produced by the first-year plant. The most delicate are those of spring, quite superior to those of autumn and winter. Early summer artichokes can also be good if they are not left to mature too much. They must be picked before the formation of the thistledown or "hairs." Harvested in a period of heat, they spoil rapidly and turn black.

Concerning the artichoke, as with everything, there are varied opinions. Although there are many who say "those of June for no one," one can find excellent canned artichokes harvested in this month.

The typical method of preparation in the Ribera is as follows: The artichokes are peeled and fixed in a way in which only the tender parts remain. They are immediately immersed in small amounts of boiling water in such a way as to avoid any rapid lowering of the water temperature. If the artichokes are made acidic by adding a little lemon or vinegar, all the better—this prevents them from turning black. The pot must be half-covered. They are done in approximately thirty minutes. They are then dried, drained, and recooked with a sauce made of bacon grease and flour lightly browned in this grease.

This recipe for artichokes should be prepared in a way so that not even a morsel is left on the plate. I believe it to be an original and unequaled recipe.

Cardoon. Cardoon is a very popular vegetable in the Ribera and little cultivated in the Cantabrian area. It is the typical vegetable of Christmas dinner in the Ribera.

Cooking is difficult, because at sea level at least two hours are needed before they are ready to eat. After cooking, a sauce made with bacon grease, flour, and garlic is added.

Asparagus

Asparagus can be grown throughout the Basque Country, but the most famous kind is produced on the alkaline soils of the Ribera de Navarra. Asparagus produced in sandy soils with a pH level around 7.5 is the best. Almost the entire quantity of canned asparagus consumed in Spain is produced in two regions—the Ribera de Navarra and the Rioja.

Asparagus is the most perishable of vegetables, as I mentioned previously. Outside of the area of production, it is almost impossible to eat it under optimal conditions. It can be well preserved, however, for twenty-four hours with water and ice. There are also excellent wild varieties, and those grown together with wheat are very tasty.

Traditionally, asparagus is eaten after being boiled. Asparagus grown among wheat is usually eaten in an omelet. In this preparation it is fried beforehand.

The popular preference is for white asparagus—the whiter the better—but it must be clarified that the green-tipped plants are excellent and perhaps tastier than the white ones.

In order to prepare this vegetable, the external fibers are removed and the asparagus is cooked in plenty of boiling water. It is eaten accompanied by a mixture of olive oil and vinegar. Asparagus must be dressed in a way that the diner can eat it without having to leave a single fiber on the plate.

Leeks

Leeks are extremely popular vegetables in the Cantabrian areas and almost unknown in the river regions. Those produced in acidic soil are the best. They are cooked alone, then eaten with potatoes. Combined with potatoes and codfish, the famous *porrusalda* stew is created—a requisite first course in many Basque areas. The leek is a principal ingredient in the blood sausages that are made on Basque farms.

The esteem for leeks is so great that it is commonly said they must be dug up with a small silver hoe.

Cabbages

Vegetables of the cabbage family are cultivated throughout the Basque Country and in almost all of their varieties: cabbages, brussels sprouts, cauliflower, etc.

The cabbages from the high regions are excellent, although the winter cabbages of the Ribera are of high quality as well. It seems that the presence of sulphur in the soil affects their quality. We have been able to note an improvement in flavor after the application of an ammonium sulfate as a fertilizer.

The cabbage and the leek are the only two vegetables that are actually popular in the Cantabrian region. Cabbages with oil (*olio-azak*) are popular in wintertime. But generally, cabbage is badly cooked in Guipúzcoa, as is the case with all vegetables.

The preparation of all cabbages must be rapid. Slightly alkaline water should be at a full boil, and the pot should be half-covered or uncovered—conditions often forgotten or not known by many *etxekoandrak* (housewives). If cabbage is cooked too long it becomes reddened and produces disagreeable odors.

A well-cooked cabbage should fully retain its original fresh color. The exception is red cabbage—its typical color is due to a pigment called anthocyanin that decomposes in an alkaline medium. Red cabbage must be cooked in acidic water with lemon or vinegar and with the lid on. The water should never be alkalized with a little bicarbonate of soda as is the case with the rest of the cabbages.

Cauliflower is harvested with a preference in the southern irrigated lands. It is usually a vegetable of high quality. For preparation we follow the same rules as for cabbage. Proceeding in this fashion we have savory, white cauliflower on our tables. Cooked cauliflower is also a Christmas dish in many houses.

Green Legumes

In this legume group we include broad beans and string beans as well as peas that are gathered long before maturity to be enjoyed because of their yet-green seeds or for their fleshy pods. They are very popular vegetables throughout the Basque Country and are consumed in enormous quantities. The best are those grown in the mild Cantabrian valleys where the soil is acidic. Those of the irrigated lands and southern dry lands are very good but are not of the quality of the former. These vegetables are eaten alone or accompanied by other vegetables, potatoes, eggs, fish, or meat.

Broad beans (*habas*) are eaten alone or accompanied by cabbage. They are also cooked and seasoned with paprika. The season for green broad beans is very short because they mature quickly through the action of the spring heat and acquire a strong taste.

In Navarra, it is the custom to eat broad beans when they have barely begun to form the seeds. The pods and seeds are cooked together without shelling. These beans are the so-called *habas con calzón.* They turn out to be very mild and have a taste very distinct from that of the shelled broad beans.

French green beans are very popular, and through the duration of the summer, they are found on the tables of all social classes. In particular, the ones called *la boz* are preferred. Other excellent varieties are almost unknown.

French green beans are eaten cooked and accompanied by potato and onion. Sometimes tomato is added. They are usually served with an uneven greenish-gray appearance. In order to retain a bright green color without losing their taste, the cooking water can be alkalized with a little bicarbonate of soda and cooked in an uncovered pot.

Tomatoes

Now a very plentiful, popular, and versatile vegetable, up until recently the tomato was used only in purées and as an accompaniment to other foods. Within a few years, its raw consumption, as in salads, has spread quickly.

The tomato of the Cantabrian area is superior to that of the Mediterranean slope. In the Ribera de Navarra, it is grown in extensive areas and destined for canning. Many of the largest canning factories in Spain are located in this region.

Its cultivation in the Cantabrian region is significantly difficult because the tomato requires a lot of heat. The lack of this element and the high humidity foster the development of cryptogamic diseases. There are years in which these fungal infections ruin the crops.

We Basques are very fond of tomato sauce, which is found in many of our typical dishes: *Lxangurro* (crab), squid, *ajo arriero* (a codfish recipe), and *tioro* (fish stew).

Peppers

Peppers are highly popular garden vegetables and are grown in many areas. All three forms—green, ripe, and dried—are widely used in our kitchens. Enormous peppers of sweet and meaty flesh are found in the Cantabrian valleys, along with small ones of delicate flesh that are picked green and then baked or fried. Many varieties of pepper are grown in the Ribera: *cristal, pico, piquillo, bola, cuerno de cabra, cuatro morros,* and others. The best are beyond a doubt the *piquillo* and *cristal* types, but they are scarce.

The famous *piperradas* are prepared with peppers. I will discuss that preparation in the section on eggs.

It is said that the pepper is indigestible, but this is true only when it is poorly prepared—an occurrence which is unfortunately all too frequent not only in private homes but also in public places. I maintain that, prepared in the following manner, they would only be indigestible to persons who have very weak gastric juices. First, the peppers are cooked over coals or on a metal kitchen griddle until the skin can be removed without force. Peppers intended for canning are usually subjected to very rapid cooking in ovens fueled by stove oil. After this baking process, the peppers made at home, as well as those in the factory, are still almost raw. It is necessary to cook them in oil for at least forty-five minutes.

To proceed correctly, minced garlic is browned in olive oil, and then the peppers are added whole or in strips. The addition of the peppers causes the temperature of the oil to rapidly decrease. The peppers emit their natural juices that, with the garlic, form an emulsion with the oil. This semiliquid bubbles at a temperature much lower than the 190° C (374° F) at which oil boils. In this way the peppers simmer more than they fry. Cooked like this and for the time designated, they form a delectable, mild, and digestible dish.

Generally, housewives brown peppers in very hot oil. The outer layers are fried and the interior remains raw, and they therefore are indigestible.

Dried peppers, called *choriceros,* are made by placing *cristal* peppers in the air and sun. These peppers are highly valued and are the basis of all "Vizcayan style" dishes.

Salad Produce

In this section I include all the garden produce that is eaten raw. The Cantabrian Basque is little given to the cultivation and consumption of this produce, but use and cultivation is nevertheless continually increasing.

I have had the opportunity to eat salads prepared with sugar instead of salt. This practice is still observed for festival banquets in outlying settlements.

My friend I. Zumalde, from Oñate, tells me that in the afternoon feast of the Octava de Corpus festival (celebrated in Oñate around the middle of the nineteenth century by the Brotherhood of the Holy Sacrament), a salad dish was always present. Excellent lettuces, endive, and chicory are grown in the Basque Country.

Chard (*acelga*) is a vegetable that adapts itself very well to all terrains and is found in all gardens. The leaves are cooked before being eaten, and the leaf ribs are rubbed with lard before cooking or served with tomato sauce.

Other Produce

In specific areas, to a greater or lesser degree, many other vegetables are grown and consumed—celery, broccoli, spinach, sorrel, salsify, squash, pumpkin, cucumbers, etc. The squashes used to prepared *pisto,* a vegetable medley that is rather popular, stand out in particular.

Onions. In other cuisines, dishes based on the onion are prepared, but among us its role never exceeds that of a complement. Still, many varieties of onions are cultivated. The basis of the Vizcayan-style sauce is formed by onions and *choricero* peppers. Our superb scallions are scarcely appreciated except in the area on the other (French) side of the Bidasoa.

Garlic. Garlic is widely grown and used. It finds its apotheosis in the fiestas of San Fermín in our ancient Iruña. During these festivals thousands of strands of garlic from Falces, Corella, and other towns are acquired by the participants.

Garlic possesses great emulgent properties in relation to fats and oils, and our cuisine takes advantage of this property in the preparation of one of its most famous sauces—*salsa verde* (green sauce). Garlic soup is also very popular. Although it is not a principal ingredient, garlic lends its name to the popular Navarrese dish of *ajo arriero,* a codfish preparation.

Carrots. Carrots never form a dish in themselves, nor are they the basis of any recipes. They are used as a seasoning in stews and in the preparation of sauces.

Herbs. Parsley is widely used and is the traditional flavoring of the *salsa verde.* Tarragon, chervil, and chives are virtually unknown in some areas but nonetheless are used commonly by the Labourdins.

Spices. The spicy element in our cooking is formed by red pepper and indigenous spices which include laurel (bay leaf), thyme, and oregano.

Concerning exotic spices which our navigators undoubtedly exposed us to, it must be noted that spices are depicted on the coat of arms of Elcano, Basque circumnavigator of the globe. Pepper, cinnamon, clove, and nutmeg are consumed with preference over the rest.

METHODS OF VEGETABLE PREPARATION

In the lines that follow I am going to briefly review some of our best methods of preparation for vegetables. There are some which are similar to others in international cuisine. These I will exclude from my narrative given that they can be found in other cookbooks.

Leek Stew (*Porrusalda*)

Leek stew is an extremely popular dish along the Cantabrian coast, mainly between the river valleys of the Deva and Nervión. There are various kinds of *porrusaldas*. The most complete is made up of leeks, potatoes, oil, and *bacalao* (salt cod). This stew is generally eaten at dinner.

Garlic Soup

Very popular in many forms, the most basic recipes for garlic soup consist of bread, oil or bacon, garlic, and *choricero* (dried) pepper. The most complete ones contain chorizo sausage, ham, eggs, etc.

Bean Stew (*Cocido*)

Consumption of bean stew, previously a popular midday dish, is declining today. In the Basque *cocido,* only the amount of water barely necessary to cook the beans should be used. In a good *cocido,* the beans should not swim in the water but rather should be surrounded by a thick, chocolate-colored soup. It is not enough, however, to merely add the correct amount of water. The beans should be of high quality and grown in the shade of cornstalks. The dry, hot years produce beans of inferior quality which are difficult to cook.

Olive oil or bacon (pork fat)—never beef lard—is added to the beans. A little chopped onion may be fried in the oil or bacon beforehand and added to the stew. If olive oil is used, it should be added when the beans are half-cooked. If bacon is used, it must be placed in the cold

water at the same time as the beans, along with any meat to be included in the stew.

Dry legumes should always be cooked in barely tepid water, in contrast to fresh vegetables. The cooking must be slow and easy. If the beans are of good quality, cooking time should last some three hours.

The complement to the *cocido* above is usually a dish of cabbage cooked in pork products. A soup is prepared from the broth of the bean stew and the cooking water of the cabbage; this serves as the first course. The beans and cabbage are eaten as the second course, and the bacon and meat of the *cocido* make up the third course.

Eltzekari

A typical *eltzekari* (a *cocido* of Labourd) is composed of cooked white beans combined with all sorts of vegetables. The fat used is usually that of pork or goose. It is a delicious dish.

Vegetable Soups (*Menestras*)

Menestras are very popular vegetable pottages of springtime. Those of the Ribera are distinguished by asparagus, those of the north by peas.

A *menestra* may include artichokes, asparagus, peas, small broad beans, new potatoes, and hearts of lettuce. Pork fat is usually used. A little ham or ham hock is also added. With the exception of lettuce and asparagus, which must be cooked beforehand, all other ingredients are cooked slowly in the fat and the liquid that is released from the vegetables themselves.

The dish *cousinette à la Bayonnaise* is a *menestra* that contains tomatoes and is flavored with white wine.

Other *Cocidos*

As has been previously mentioned, the consumption of dried broad beans has almost been abandoned. The fat used to accompany them is usually lard, which woodcutters used to salt to ensure preservation.

The consumption of garbanzos is not very extensive. They are used, however, in the preparation of the so-called *caldo limpio* (bouillon). The garbanzos are cooked with meat, carrot, parsley, chorizo, and bacon. The broth which remains after cooking is the *caldo limpio*. Garbanzos are not overly popular, but during Lent, more of them are eaten, together with spinach or chard.

Dried peas and lentils are eaten on a very small scale.

Seasoned Croutons

Croutons, very popular among Navarrese shepherds, are easily prepared. *Pan sobado,* a traditional dense Spanish bread, is cut into cubes. The cubes are cooked slowly in mutton fat to which red pepper is added. It is very common to leave the bread cubes to soak overnight before frying. There is a variation in which the croutons are soaked in milk. In this case red pepper is not added.

3

MEATS AND POULTRY

BIRDS AND MAMMALS

TODAY few species of birds and mammals enter into our diet on a regular basis. Their identification is quite easy, with the exception of birds about which exists some confusion because of an inaccurate taxonomic classification. I will not apply scientific names here with as much rigor as I will in the section on fishes. Only when some doubt arises will I even include the scientific name.

It seems beyond doubt that hunting constituted one of man's first activities on earth. Even today there are still primitive tribes that devote their major efforts to hunting.

Animals provided by hunting were at times plentiful and at other times scarce. This irregularity of a meat supply was minimized to a large extent by the domestication of animals. Perhaps beginning with the capture of a wounded beast or animal of smaller size, man realized that he could raise them at will in the proximity of human settlements. A similar thing may have occurred with birds which were quite easy to capture in an infantile state in their nests.

The mammals in captivity regularly provided meat, skins, bones, and entrails; man also began to procure blood and milk from them. Later, as Telesforo de Aranzadi so aptly said, man invented the ox as a beast of burden. From that time on he used this strong and docile "invention" for labor and transportation.

Man, who in the beginning indiscriminately ate all kinds of mammals, must have realized that the herbivores were not only more susceptible to domestication but also provided more flavorful meat and gave abundant milk. In addition, the feeding of herbivores was very simple.

THE QUALITY OF OUR MEATS

The animals raised in the Basque Country, when well nourished, produce meat which equals that of any other region.

With beef, the preferred meat is that of young animals—about one year old and weighing 200 to 300 kilos (90 to 135 pounds) on the hoof. Veal is not highly valued and with good reason. It is very tender meat but has little flavor, and we feel it is more appropriate for the delicate and the sick.

The best meat is from sterile calves. For reasons which I will not enumerate in this book, our farms produce a relatively high number of these calves (*machorras*) which cannot be induced to grow to maturity. The farmer usually takes them to the butcher after their sterility is proven

through many tests. They are usually three years old, fat, and superbly developed. Their meat is typically exceptional.

The ox, rapidly disappearing in the Basque region today, has not been raised for meat in the same way as in Galicia or France. The ones that were slaughtered were usually old and overworked. A butchered cow, with the exception of some unforeseen sacrifice, was usually old and in poor condition.

Wool-bearing animals are highly regarded as a meat source in the Basque Country. Mutton, however, is not widely accepted along the Cantabrian coast. In Navarra much sheep is eaten, and lambs between six months and one year old are usually quite good. The castration of the lambs is an almost forgotten practice. When castration is done, however, a meat results which rivals the best French *moutons*.

Suckling lamb (*arkume, ternasco*) is valued throughout the area. Most are excellent, but to my taste, the southern part of Vitoria (the area of Treviño) is where the best ones are raised. "Twin" lambs, or those raised with the milk of two sheep, are also exceptional.

Little goat meat is eaten now that the animals are not commonly found in the Basque region. Suckling goats are usually very good.

Pork is raised throughout the Basque Country and is usually of good quality but is not special in any particular respect.

Whale meat was widely eaten long ago—our ancestors were fishermen of these great mammals. In the same way that the whales have practically disappeared from our seas, their meat has virtually vanished from our kitchens without a trace.

Large mammals such as deer, Pyrenean chamois, wild boar, etc., have almost ceased to exist in our forests, and as a consequence the same thing has happened as with the whale, in that all recipes for such meats

have disappeared. When one of these animals is accidentally captured, it is prepared according to international recipes or simply treated as any other meat.

We have an aversion to eating horse meat, but with the increased food prices, places where horse meat can be bought have become more common. It seems that its consumption is gradually increasing because it is so economical.

Rodents are represented by the hare, the mountain rabbit, and the domesticated rabbit, the first two being of high quality and having great popularity.

Fowl are good sources of meat. Due to an incomprehensible neglect the old breed of chickens—once found on our farms, which produced incomparable specimens—is dying off. Hunting is gradually disappearing, but quail, partridge, woodcock, etc., are usually quite good.

METHODS OF MEAT PREPARATION

Primitive man must have eaten meat raw; perhaps later he learned to cure it. With the use of fire he ate roasted meat. The invention of pottery allowed meat to be boiled. Stews would have been developed later on by associating meat with vegetable products obtained by the women through cultivation or by collection in the forests.

So that the reader will be aware of the various processes of roasting, boiling, and stewing, I will provide an explanation of those methods in a manner following the technical style used by the author Eduard de Pomiane. My discussion will be arranged in an unorthodox manner. In most cookbooks the author will speak of veal, for example, and then provide all of its various recipes. Here I will talk first about the method—roasting, for example—and then I will discuss all the species of mammals and fowl that are prepared in that manner.

Roasting

Primitive man roasted whole pieces of meat over bonfires or hot coals. We have already seen in the first part of this book the way in which, even today, Australian aborigines prepare kangaroo. One version of this practice is the common one in the Basque Country of bleeding, then burning a pig carcass. We do not allow it to complete cooking but rather interrupt the operation when the pig is singed and the hooves can be easily removed.

Roasting should be quite elemental. The piece of meat to be roasted should have enough of its own fat to prevent it from drying out during cooking. The addition of other animal fats is unnatural. If the meat does not have a sufficient quantity of its own fat, it should not be roasted and should be used instead in recipes that take advantage of leanness.

Roasting is a fairly expensive but superb procedure. It is expensive because there is no recuperation of fats and juices that fall from the meat to burn up on the coals below. It is unsurpassed because these same juices and fats, on burning, produce aromatic smoke that rises and seasons the meat to perfection.

If a beast is roasted with its skin intact, the skin acts as a protective cover and prevents loss of muscle plasma. If on the contrary, the meat is exposed without skin to the heat of the live coals, the albumins coagulate and the carbohydrates caramelize, forming a protective cover that prevents the drying of the meat.

Large pieces, skewered or attached to sticks, are placed over the fire at a variable distance. In this way heat enters the meat through radiation and convection. This is the basis of our roast, the *burruntzi*, which has been so popular in the Basque Country the last few years. It is the ideal procedure to roast good meat.

If the skewer on which the meat is suspended is placed in a vertical position near the bonfire, instead of horizontally, the piece of meat will only receive heat through radiation. Although the bonfire gives off quite a lot of smoke, the smoke will not affect the meat as much, since it rises in a direction parallel to the spit. This is a procedure widely used by the natives of South America.

Employing these systems, and given that meat is a poor conductor of heat, the meat must be rotated to achieve uniformity in cooking. This, in short, is the manner of roasting that, from the dark and distant days of prehistory, continues to be practiced today, even though it is no longer a common occurrence. This basic and simple procedure has not been even remotely equalled by later techniques.

Roasting in clay casseroles, in bread ovens, and in modern kitchen ovens using the most varied sources of heat—coal, gas, petroleum, and electricity—has simplified operations and given regularity to the products, but these methods do not achieve a flavor as agreeable as that of meat roasted over coals.

Brillat-Savarin has said that the chef is made and the barbecuer or roaster is born. In a strictly literal sense this is a blatant exaggeration, but the roaster must have better powers of observation than the chef. The intensity of the fire, the correct distance, and the quality and size of the roast are important considerations in attaining perfect preparations.

Errors committed in barbecuing cannot be remedied. The roast appears as nude on the table as Venus from the sea. There cannot be even the slightest defect, for the most unsophisticated eater will notice it. A stew permits alterations, additions, and cosmetic remedies that cannot be applied to roasted or grilled meat.

If the meat is cut into steaks, the spit then becomes an inadequate instrument. This difficulty is solved by the use of a grill. Today grills are

widely used for the cooking of fish and chops. The spit, more difficult to manage, is almost obsolete.

Two instruments have been responsible for the spit falling into disuse. With the aim of bringing convenience to our housewives, the modern stove and the frying pan have also produced a decrease in the quality of the prepared meats we eat.

The modern stove has retired the fireplaces that were used for cooking in homes and fueled by firewood or charcoal. The skillet has provided for easy frying and cooking in oil. In an oil solution, the temperature is better regulated and the meat therefore prevented from burning or being underdone. From the point of view of convenience and economy, frying pans and stoves are admirable for roasting meat, but from a gastronomic perspective, we can qualify this convenience as being an ill-fated one.

The English, great masters of roasting, cook enormous pieces of meat which weigh many pounds. Generally these hunks belong to the part of the carcass which we call "the chop belt." We generally eat pieces from this section that have been cut transversely. A good chop should weight at least 350 grams (12 ounces) if we wish to grill it. Considering that today the chop roasted on a grill is the genuine representation of ancient practice, I will review its preparation in a place where the roasting of it is almost a ritual.

The Chops of Azpeitia. The area of Azpeitia is a marvelous enclave in our small province of Guipúzcoa. Industrialization has still not marred the perfection of its countryside. The climate is mild, humid, and temperate. The sprawling farms are found nestled between meadows, fern fields, and woods. The soil is fresh, fertile, and deep. A mountain barrier encloses all of the valley, leaving only two narrow openings through which the Urola River enters and exits the lowland.

Within the valley, the Urola receives abundant and pure waters that cleanse it of the pollutants which it receives from my hometown.

On this land magnificent animals are raised that are descendants of an ancient Pyrenean breed. The cows produce an abundance of milk, and often the surplus is difficult to sell. For this reason, on the farms far from the highways or urban centers, calves can suckle the ample and fatty milk of their mothers until the pending arrival of a sibling dries up the udder. With abundant milk in the first few months, followed by a diet of plentiful and succulent grass, it is not surprising that splendid animals are produced.

It is a shame that these calves cannot claim to be of a pure Pyrenean lineage. I believe that if we would have devoted as much attention to our native breeds as the English have done, we would have a meat-producing strain today that would be the equal of many types raised outside our country. The truth is that we have diluted the bloodline with importations of new breeds, and now we do not know what will become of our livestock.

Nevertheless, sound nutrition can be more important than lineage, and the calves raised in the area of Azpeitia do grow up robust and ample. When they are twelve months old, they are taken to the butcher. Here their beauty always inspires admiration that is converted into wagers on the weight of their carcasses. Azpeitia is a town of gamblers, and they bet on the weights of the domestic livestock as well as on the outcome of the tests of strength held in the town's spacious plaza where animals are pitted against one another (rams, oxen, etc.).

After the carcass has left the slaughterhouse, it will remain in the butcher shop about ten days—in winter, fifteen. Then the butcher will cut chops weighing about 500 to 700 grams (18 to 25 ounces) each.

With these chops we will continue on to the Aitzaki restaurant. Dozens and dozens of chops are roasted there daily, and, once in a while, several hundred are prepared.

A small pile of charcoal is lit. When the smouldering pieces are burning well, they are spread out. A large grill is placed over the coals. When the iron bars are quite hot, they are cleaned with brown paper. As the blue flames of the charcoal begin to disappear, the chop is placed on the grill. Sizzling then occurs as it cooks. Let us examine the procedure in detail: The subtle crackling of the meat continues, but soon we will notice, on the side of the chop away from the fire, rosy red spots of plasma which ideally appear over the whole chop. At this time the meat is turned and the cooking continues. Again, droplets of plasma will appear on the roasted side. We wait a little longer, since the fire has lost some of its heat.

Now we have the chop on the plate. Both sides are evenly browned, without black or white spots, and it exudes a delicious aroma. Little else is on the table—a place setting of a knife and fork, good bread, and Rioja wine.

We begin to eat the chop in a way which we could call *por cola* (by the tail). The main deposit of fat is found at the narrow end, and this must be eaten while very hot. The feast is continued along the outside edge which is also fatty. The meat should be rosy-colored in the middle; its texture should be granular, and its aroma should make our mouths water. It is not necessary to eat this meat very hot because it is just as good lukewarm or even cold.

At the end, we have no reservations about picking up the bone in our hands and tearing off the delicious remains with our teeth. When the bones are cleaned, we ask for a good cheese from Urbía, Aralar, or Urbasa.

With these four basic elements—meat, bread, wine, and cheese—

we will have partaken of a very primitive type of meal, but I do not believe one could find greater satisfaction in the eating of a three-course feast.

For my taste, this form of preparation is incomparable. Of course, excellent roast meats are prepared in other Basque towns.

As regards the size of the chops, we stumble upon an almost moral problem. "Monogamy" must be practiced with the chop—one meat chop solely intended for each diner's enjoyment from beginning to end. "Polygamy," or the serving of two or more chops to each dinner guest, is inappropriate.

Nor do I accept "polyandry," produced when the chop is cut up in hunks and divided among the guests. The technique employed in the preparation of English roast beef is such a form of polyandry, given that enormous pieces of meat, whole sides of chops from oxen or beef, are roasted and then sliced.

We could almost say that the moral influence of the Guipuzcoan St. Ignatius de Loyola had even reached the grills of Aitzaki in his native town of Azpeitia.

Some months ago I had the opportunity to eat at the Simpson restaurant in London. In his book *La casa de Lúculo,* Camba praises the Simpson in a manner for which the establishment could never pay him. The form of preparing and serving meat is described by Camba with the precision of a Benedictine liturgy.

> They served the enormous piece of roasted meat, taken from the best animals of the world and prepared by a centuries' old technique.
>
> Bread and beer were served in silver containers. The garnish was very simple: steamed potatoes and boiled cabbage. Before me,

the carver stood, ready to carve the meat and to receive a tip for the task.

Everything was delicious, difficult to improve upon, but I, who am not a chauvinist, was mentally transported to Aitzaki and its chops were evoked, for its meat was a worthy competitor of that which I now had before me.

Aitzaki: Old, traditional restaurant where meals are served with magnificent simplicity. There it is easy to fantasize about the foods of an ancient people.

Roast lamb. Roasting a whole lamb over coals, using the spit, is much more complicated than roasting steaks and chops. Lamb meat is very irregular in thickness. The hindquarter has greater masses of meat, the front less so, and the center is very lean except in the area surrounding the kidneys.

The process is slow and difficult to explain in detail. To prevent the drying out of the meat during the hour in which it is roasted, it is rubbed with bacon grease or basted with vinegar and garlic.

I have seen lamb roasted to perfection at the Acitain restaurant in Eibar. The cook, Pablo Aguirre, is a master not only of roasting but also of serving. He divides the pieces among the eaters according to their physiognomy. One who has a face indicating a small appetite is given ribs; the guest who appears to be used to sumptuous meals is given the fatty pieces to "strain the stomach," according to Aguirre's expression. Details of this kind should be noticed by many maitre d's and waiters who usually note nothing more than what their clients order.

In the Ribera region of Navarra, many lamb chops are roasted on a grill and flavored with garlic and parsley. They are truly magnificent.

Roast suckling pigs. Suckling pigs are very young piglets that are highly valued in the area of Navarra. The roasting should take place slowly so that the fat flows. It they are roasted over a high heat, they will brown too quickly, resulting in large quantities of fatty tissue that make the meat indigestible.

I have not seen suckling pigs cooked on the *burruntzi*. The best way to cook them is in a baker's oven.

Francisco Javier Arraiza provides two curious details about suckling pigs in his book *La cocina navarra.* The suckling pig should have a nut in its mouth as it roasts, and once it is roasted, it should not be placed in any light. Therefore, one must curtain the kitchen and dining room windows and eat in near darkness.

Quail in fig leaves. Quail are wrapped in fig leaves greased with pork lard, and bacon strips are placed on top of the leaves. Then they are roasted on the spit (*burruntzi*) or in the oven.

Chops Bilbao style. Chops are prepared with garlic, parsley, and bread crumbs and then grilled. They should be rare on the inside. The classic garnish is green or red peppers.

Capón al burruntzi. Very young, fat capons are required. Without a doubt spit roasting is the best method of preparing these fowl.

Boiling, Stewing, and Frying

The invention of pottery permitted foods to be boiled in water or in oil. Meat, when grilled, loses a large quantity of oils and liquids which drop on the coals. The loss is not total in that as these products burn, they infiltrate the meat and, with the charcoal, lend their unmistakable taste to the meat. However, there is undoubtedly a great weight loss to the roast.

In boiling, the meat substances are not lost due to the action of the heat because they combine with the cooking liquid to form a broth.

We get different results from boiling, depending on whether we submerge the meat in cold water or boiling water. If we begin with meat added to cold water and placed over the heat, after a prolonged cooking we will have a flavorful broth and a relatively tasteless, stringy, and fibrous meat. If we add garden vegetables to this we have "invented the stew."

On the other hand, if we submerge the meat in salted water at a full boil, in the end we will have a flavorful and firm meat and a bland broth.

If we place the meat in a tightly closed pot, accompanied by vegetables, spices, herbs, or wine, after about three hours of cooking we will have a covered "oven" stew (an *estofado*).

If we submerge the meat in an open pot in very hot grease, we will have a fried dish. The difference between something "boiled" or something "fried" rests simply in the temperatures at which boiling takes place in each of the cooking solutions. In water, in standard pots, the temperature will not rise above 100° C (212° F) whereas in a frying pan 200° C (418° F) can be reached.

After having fried meat, we can create a good sauce by adding onions, garlic, carrots, flour, and herbs to the remaining fat in the pan and diluting it with a bit of water. If the fried meat continues to cook in this sauce, we end up with a stew.

Stew Bilbao style. This stew (*menestra*) is a mixture of artichokes, hearts of lettuce, small potatoes, peas, mushrooms, and asparagus, along with sweetbreads and ham.

Calves' tongue with nuts. The tongue is stuffed with bacon, garlic, crackers, and walnuts. The sauce is made and strained through a colander. It is then poured over the tongue slices and the dish is served.

Tolosan tongue. Tongue is cooked in a medley of vegetables. Once cooked, it is cut into slices that are dipped in egg and fried. A purée is made with the cooked vegetables and flavored with white wine. A sauce is made with this purée, and the slices of tongue are simmered in it for half an hour.

Tripe of the market (callos al ferial). Tripe is cleaned and partially cooked. Chorizo, ham, and onion are fried slowly in olive oil and then added to the tripe. The preparation is completed by boiling the entire mixture. The dish should be spicy.

Tripe Vizcayan style. Cleaned and cooked tripe is served in the same sauce used in the preparation of cod *a la vizcaina.*

Hog snouts Vizcayan style. The recipe for hog snouts is quite similar to that of tripe Vizcayan style.

Pork loin in milk. This recipe for pork loin is both excellent and original. The loin is cooked in a small quantity of milk for about one hour. The milk turns into a creamy white sauce and is seasoned to taste.

Pork chops in red wine. The pork chops are fried, and a thick sauce is made with garlic, parsley, bread crumbs, and red wine. This sauce is cooked until it holds together well and is then added to the chops.

Lamb al chilindrón. Four front quarters of lamb are cut up, fried, and cooked in a purée made of tomatoes and *choricero* peppers. Strips of sweet peppers are added. On serving, the dish is sprinkled with garlic and chopped parsley.

Lamb stew. This *menestra* begins with a vegetable mixture to which fried lamb is added. They are cooked together until the lamb is tender.

Lamb chops Guipuzcoan style. Fried chops are cooked with browned onion, potatoes, broth, and cider. Pepper, laurel, parsley, and cloves are added as spices.

Lamb sweetbreads in golden sauce. Lamb sweetbreads are cooked in broth and are served with a sauce made with lard (or butter), ham, flour, and broth.

Stuffed squash (calabacín). The squash is cleaned out and refilled with a ground meat mixture. It is dipped in egg and rolled in flour and then cooked in a sauce made with onion, carrot, flour, and white wine.

Stuffed peppers. The recipe for stuffed peppers is very similar to the one for stuffed squash.

Rabbit with peppers. Pieces of rabbit are prepared in the oven with roasted peppers, a little water, salt, and spices.

Chicken in tomato sauce. Very young chickens (pullets) are killed and are cut into pieces, fried, and served with a tomato purée.

Chicken a la Irouleguy. This chicken dish is very similar to the chicken in tomato sauce. Bayonne ham and Basque wine from Irouleguy are added to the sauce.

Chicken al chilindrón. This chicken recipe is the same as that for lamb *al chilindrón.*

Preserved goose (confitura de ganso, confit d'ote). The goose is quartered and cooked in a mixture of oil and goose fat and then preserved in the strained goose fat within a large earthenware jar. It is a superb dish.

Small wild birds (chimbos). The birds are fried in oil or butter and set aside. Bread crumbs, garlic, and chopped parsley are fried in the remaining fat, and then this hot mixture is poured over the cooked birds.

I believe I have covered the different fundamental ways in which meat is prepared. Meat can be preserved by some basic physical and chemical procedures—salting, smoking, and dehydration are processes that humanity has employed since time immemorial.

Sausages and Cured Meats

Chorizos (Basque sausages) are made of meat and pork fat seasoned with paprika, salt, and garlic. The sausage is then stuffed into casings and dried.

Throughout the Basque Country, excellent chorizos of different types are produced. Those from Pamplona enjoy a well-deserved fame. There are various kinds of *longaniza* (*txistor* in Basque) which are eaten fried. The *sabadeños* (*birikiak*) are eaten half-dried and cooked in a pot of beans and are quite good.

Hams are cured, but they never attain the quality of those made in the Andalucian mountains. If curing occurs without an excess of salt, good hams are produced. The hams of Bayonne and Navarra are famous in France. A magnificent dish called *magras a la Navarra* is made with desalted slices of ham which are fried and served with a tomato purée.

It is a common practice to preserve dried tongue and pigs feet after treating them in a salt bath.

On the farms, dried meat (*cecina, zezina*), which was eaten in stews, was once quite common, but it is hardly eaten anymore.

In the Basque lands beyond the Bidasoa (in France), there are masters of the preservation of fried goose in its own fat. This is what constitutes the exquisite *confit d'oie.*

THE USE OF BLOOD IN BASQUE COOKING

In the first part of this book, in the section called Prehistory, I talked about primitive ways of killing animals and preparing them for eating. I noted that the blood is the first part of the animal to be used, along with some of the entrails. Some of these methods have persisted into modern times in the Basque Country.

Since early times blood has been consumed by man, as much in the observance of religious and superstitious practices as for simple nutrition.

Basques of the rural areas are very given to the consumption of blood, and its preparation is almost a ritual for them. The day of the pig butchering—a main source of blood in our cooking—is usually a full-fledged day of celebration on Basque farms.

From determining the day of the sacrifice (based on the moon's phases) to the preparation of the blood or meat sausages, family and local traditions are observed, and an atmosphere of an earlier time pervades the house.

Generally, the presence of foods prepared with blood presupposes at least a temporary abundance of food, considering that blood represents only a small part of the bulk of a slaughtered animal. But the consumption of these foods has not always occurred in times of prosperity. Arocena shared with me the following excerpt from *Las Bienandanzas e fortunas* by Lope García de Salazar (1399–1476):

> In the year of our Lord MCCCXLIII, in Castilla and León, during the reign of good king Don Alfonso, last of this name, there was considerable drought in the land and, because of their sins, many people died of hunger, walking along the roads and dropping dead muttering, "Give me bread." And they bled the cattle through the main arteries because they were not suitable for eating . . . and they cooked the blood in cauldrons and ate it coagulated and cooked it in slices with salt. And the elders say that to their recollection those who died were sailors and blacksmiths and coal workers and officials that were experts in showing off, and that the others that were used to eating moderately endured their hunger better and so be it that God aided them.

This statement informs us not only of a sad epoch in our history but also of the professions that were distinguished by their voracity.

Today blood is not eaten in coagulated form. Generally, it is consumed in the form of blood sausage (made of lamb or pork), in an omelet with tripe and eggs, and as a complement to the preparation of rabbit.

Blood Sausages (*Morcillas*)

It seems that our blood sausages originated in Asia and were introduced in Europe by the Phoenicians. In medieval documents, the references to *morcillas* are frequent.

Dr. Joubert gives a recipe for the preparation of *morcillas* in France in the sixteenth century. Blood, thyme, fennel, marjoram, parsley, hyssop, and various other spices entered into the preparation, with the exception of savory. This is not used because its addition would prevent the coagulation of the blood. Fresh savory, in fact, is used to dissolve the clots of blood which originate in the veins.

In the Basque Country, not only does each region or each zone have its particular method of preparation, but individual towns and families jealously guard their own traditional recipes for blood sausages. In Navarra and Alava, rice is used as a stuffing and complement to the fat and blood, whereas in Guipúzcoa and parts of Vizcaya, this complement is provided by thoroughly cooked onions and leeks.

Generally, the *morcillas* are made of blood and pork fat and are called *odolkiak* or *odolosteak* in Basque. We have already noted that those made of blood and lamb fat, very popular in the Goierri region, are called *buzkantzak* or *mondejus.* These are stronger but more flavorful than those made of pork.

In that these recipes for blood sausage are quite adulterated by tavern keepers, and considering that their preparation in homes is becoming increasingly rare, I have included the method of preparation for *buzkantzak* used by my late aunt, Juana Busca Sagastizabal, in the recipe section. Over the last hundred years, this recipe has not had even one minor modification.

Following this recipe with care can guarantee not only excellence in the dish but also easy digestibility. Blood sausages are usually criticized for being difficult to digest. This may be due to the fat or the filling, because, in fact, cooked blood is digested quite well. If the sausage does not contain too much fat and is from a young animal, a healthy person can digest it without difficulty. To my knowledge, the onions and leeks are generally introduced not thoroughly cooked and therefore are not easy to digest. To me, the success of either *morcillas* or *buzkantzak* lies in the proper cooking of the leeks and onions.

Frikatza

In our cooking there exists a link between blood and the intestines that is clearly seen in the *frikatza*. The intestines of the suckling lamb are not strong enough for stuffing. The lamb's blood is collected upon butchering of the animal and coagulates in a mold for cooking. The intestines are cooked and cut up. The blood, also cut up, is fried with onion and the intestines. It is then added to beaten eggs. This is a typical spring meal, spring being the best season for suckling lamb.

Civet of hare

I will not explain civet here but rather make note that blood is an important ingredient in the sauce of this ragout. The recipe belongs to international cooking, but here the chefs, who have no complete knowledge of other cuisines, invariably prepare rabbit in its own blood.

FROGS AND REPTILES

The frog (*Rana esculenta*)—*rana* in Spanish, *igel* in Basque—is the only edible representative among the species of amphibians. They are much more valued along the Mediterranean slope than in the Cantabrian zone. Their meat is fine, very white, and has an excellent flavor.

Generally, the meaty legs are the only part eaten, although in many places frogs are served whole after they have been skinned and gutted.

Fried frog legs. The frog legs are skinned and cleaned, then rolled in a frying batter. They are fried in plenty of oil which should be very hot.

Frogs in tomato sauce. This is a very popular recipe in the Ribera. Once the frogs have been fried, a tomato purée is added to them and they are simmered for half an hour.

Frogs a la Rochapea. This is a frog leg recipe by Francisco Javier Arraiza. Mushrooms, parsley, onion, clove, garlic, and lard are used in addition to broth and white wine. The sauce is thickened with bread crumbs and egg yolks.

Reptiles are not typically included in our meals. On the contrary, consumption of them is exceptional. Nevertheless, some species of lizards and snakes are cooked in and eaten from *calderillos* or *ranchos,* large pots used to prepare dishes outdoors. I have no knowledge of tortoises or turtles having been eaten. On occasion, however, Basque fishermen have caught sea turtles. It is probable that they could belong to some excellent species like that used in the famous English soup.

4

FISH AND SEAFOOD

ON beginning this part of my book, we enter into its most distinguished section. It is with seafood that our chefs have accomplished their most delicious, attractive, and original recipes.

Despite the unquestionable reputation of French cuisine, one can point to the apparent scarcity of recipes for ocean fish, with the exception of sole. The preference of our neighbors for terrestrial foods also seems to reflect this paucity.

Basques—many of them sailors and fishermen—have always prepared their dishes with the utmost care. From this comes the unsurpassable repertory of fish dishes, unique and beyond compare.

The turbulent waters of our coasts produce an infinity of species

with excellent culinary qualities. These intermediate waters, between the cold northern ones and the temperate southerly ones, seem to supply the best conditions for the nurturing of the species. The fish do not reach gigantic sizes, as in other waters, but they stand out because of the excellence of their meat. It is a phenomenon similar to that occurring in the plant kingdom, in that many fruits and vegetables reach their maximum flavor in certain zones. Along our coasts we have beaches and cliffs, shallow and deep waters. There are also rivers of intermediate salinity at their lower ends.

The Basque for some centuries has been a lover of the sea, and he treats all that pertains to it with affection—navigation, war, shipping, and fishing. In addition, foods from the sea are prepared with more care than foods of agricultural origin. However, the Basques of the interior, despite having excellent river fish at their disposal, have not produced any original dishes that make use of them.

We eat fish in all forms imaginable, with the exception of raw or smoked preparations. It is odd that smoked fish, so popular and excellent among the Nordic countries, is not consumed by us. It is even more curious that this is true when, in fact, our fishermen are very fond of the excellent smoked cheeses made by Basque shepherds.

Before getting on with the subject at hand I wish to make a note concerning the format of this section. Given the vast variety of seafood species included and the various names they receive in different ports, I am going to attempt to establish a systematic approach so that each species is always clearly defined. However, in some instances I will have to leave things without clarification.

Whenever it is possible, I will provide first the English name, then the scientific one, followed by the Spanish term, and finally, the Basque

designation. In this way, I hope to avoid the confusion that is created in many cookbooks.

MOLLUSKS

There are numerous edible species in the mollusk group—some of which, appropriately prepared, play a major role in the most typical Basque cuisine.

Octopus and Squid

The octopus (*Octopus vulgaris*) is very plentiful on our coasts. It is called *pulpo* in Spanish and *olagarro* in Basque. This mollusk is an insatiable devourer of crabs, small fish, and clams. It possesses great strength and, using its suction cups, is able to open clams and other bivalves. The octopus kills its prey with a poison produced from its posterior salivary glands. The squid also kills its quarry in this manner.

Octopus meat is tough and leathery but is very flavorful. It is easily preserved through drying and consumed during periods of limited food supply.

Octopus, either fresh or dried, is often used in soups. Before cooking, the octopus should be soaked to tenderize its tough meat by placing it in a sauce of oil and vegetables. (If dried octopus is used, it must be left to soak for several hours.) After some three hours, water is added. All the mixture is then boiled and at the end, slices of bread are added. The end result is a soup that is flavorful but very strong.

Small octopus can be eaten fried or baked without previous preparation. Stews are also made with octopus accompanied by potatoes and peppers. Dishes made from octopus are always strong tasting, but once the palate becomes accustomed to the flavor, they are eaten with gusto.

The European squid (*Loligo vulgaris, calamar, txipiroi*) is one of the most unusual inhabitants of our seas. It has captured the imagination of fishermen, and there are tales that tell of "inkfish" so gigantic they have been confused with islands. Legend has it that on one occasion, Mass was said on the back of a gigantic squid.

In reality, enormous squids do exist, but they do not reach the size of the fabled ones. Some specimens of around 12 meters (39 feet) in length (including the tentacles) and about 2 meters (6½ feet) in circumference have been captured. We are horrified at the idea of considering such a giant animal as a meal; consequently we prefer the small squid.

A very characteristic feature of these animals is that they are able to maneuver by jet propulsion, projecting water out of the interior mantle cavity of their bodies against the surrounding water. The force is sometimes so great that it permits the animal to make long leaps over the surface of the sea.

The squid is a creature in which mimicry finds its greatest example. Compared to this cephalopod, the terrestrial chameleon is a mere apprentice. The squid's body is provided with numerous chromatophores which allow it to adapt the color of its body to that of its surroundings with incredible speed. These pigment-containing cells can be clearly observed in freshly caught specimens. These cells on the outer surface of the squid can expand and contract for a certain amount of time after death.

The name "calamary" comes from the Latin *calamario,* or ink-maker, and curiously, within the squid is a chitinous shell or quill. By cutting up this quill and dipping it in the ink of the squid itself, one can write perfectly well.

The Basques have prepared some of their most famous culinary creations with the squid. The color of a dish is of fundamental importance to the sighted eater. The great cooks possess the rare ability of serving chromatically harmonized dishes. In the preparation of squid with an ink sauce, the problems of serving a black-colored dish must be confronted. Many inland people reject this preparation without even trying it simply because of its appearance.

The great Pomiane, speaking of the color black in food preparation, says, "Black is left to us yet: the truffle and the black olive are rare examples of this color that is the negation of color."

The foods that Pomiane mentions do not in themselves constitute complete dishes. Leaving aside black olives because of their limited culinary application, it would seem we are left with only the expensive truffle, used as a complement because of its aroma and color. While the aroma may dominate the preparation, the truffle's color is only for contrast with the lightest colors.

The sauce prepared for the squid, however, is of an absolutely black color, so dark that even the white body of the squid itself seems blackened. The color contrast of the dish is achieved with pieces of golden fried bread, resulting in a curiously bright yet somber appearance. The boldness of this plate is not limited to its color. The ink of the squid that blackens and flavors the dish is stored in a sac located near the anal orifice. This ink, in addition to having such black properties, is also toxic when fresh. However, the mild toxicity of the fresh ink is eliminated by the action of heat. Even in its crude, poisonous state, its toxic action for larger animals does not seem so great. Cats, who are very fond of snatching away the ink sacks of the squid, do not suffer any major difficulties in digesting them.

There are various recipes to prepare squid in its own ink. It is not necessary to add more than basic seasonings for flavor and consistency of the sauce, because the animal itself possesses sufficient flavor.

The squid are stuffed with their own tentacles, fried, and then slowly simmered in a sauce made of onion, tomato purée, and the ink. A little parsley, cayenne pepper, and some black pepper may be added. This dish is accompanied by the fried bread slices already mentioned.

Each cook has his own recipe which is more or less secret. The essential element, however, is very fresh squid of small size caught with a lure and not a net. The difference between the animals captured by the two methods lies in the treatment they receive. Soon after being caught, the hooked animals are put in a clean basket with great care and arrive at the market in a few hours. The loss of ink is minimum and the bodies are left without contusions or scrapes. Squids caught with a net become macerated among the other fish, lose their ink, and in general do not reach the market for several days.

In some ports squids are grilled and are excellent when prepared in this way. The consumption of fried squid in the style of the Mediterranean coast is spreading, particularly in taverns.

The cuttlefish (*Sepia officinalis, sepia, pota*) is a near relative of the squid, but its meat and flavor are far inferior, and the color of its ink is not black, but dark brown. This mollusk has provided art and industry with a color called sepia which is made from its ink.

Cuttlefish is prepared in the same way as squid and, to the untutored diner, served as if it were identical.

Snails

Within the snail group we find both terrestrial and marine animals.

The limpet (*Patella vulgata*), called *lapa* in both Spanish and Basque, is very plentiful along our coasts. Its meat is tough and leathery and for this reason is not highly appreciated. It is eaten only along the coastal zones. Limpets are usually prepared in a manner similar to that used for clams, but the most common dish is a soup. Once thoroughly cleaned, limpets are boiled in water, salt, vegetables, and *chacolí* (a white wine). A soup is made with the broth, the limpet meat, and bread or rice.

The lined monodont (*Monodonta lineata, bígaro, karrakela*) is a small snail found along our escarpments. It is eaten simply, prepared in salted water. A needle must be employed to extract the meat from the shell. It is used as an appetizer rather than as a main dish.

Terrestrial snails. I should make a place here in these pages for the snails that occupy our countryside, since I find no more appropriate place in this book to include them. These are mollusks adapted to the respiration of air, but they have a structure very similar to that of sea snails.

It seems as if the ancient Basques were not very fond of eating land snails. As I mentioned in the first chapter, Father Barandiarán considers the helicophobia of our rural people today to be a holdover from pre-historic times. Nonetheless, in many urban areas now, people are quite fond of snails. Consumption of these animals almost constitutes a ritual, and there are days designated for the partaking of snails: Christmas, Holy Thursday, St. Andrew's Day, etc. Along the Basque Mediterranean slope, they are eaten by everyone and even play a role in *calderillos*, the pots of food prepared in the countryside. I have seen furtive snail gatherers grill and eat them immediately upon collection.

The majority of edible snails belong to the genus *Helix* and are called *caracoles* in Spanish, *kurkuilloak* in Basque. Historically, they were a favorite dish of the Romans, who raised them in large quantities.

Ignacio Domenech's book *La cocina vasca* includes a recipe from an excellent Basque gourmet, Juan de Irigoyen. The recipe consists of two parts: one dealing with the cooking of the snails and the other with preparing the sauce. The snails are cooked in a tasty broth of vegetables.

The sauce is made of fresh olive oil, onion, bacon, and *choricero* pepper pulp. The latter is a fine preparation that is also used in making the sauces of our most typical dishes.

Given the almost ritualistic nature of the eating of snails, there are probably some distinctive recipes from each town. From the ethnographic point of view as much as from the gastronomic, it would prove most interesting to compile them.

Bivalves

Many varieties of bivalves are used in our cooking. The mussel (*Mytilus edulis, mejillón, muskullu*) is very plentiful and has been eaten by Basques since prehistoric times. Today it is not very popular, and most of the harvest is exported. Mussels are raised in Galicia and Cataluña, but commercial cultivation is not practiced in the Basque region.

The oyster (*Ostrea edulis, ostra, ispel*) abounds on our coasts but is not cultivated. Our oysters are inferior in quality to those on the coasts of Galicia and Marennes, which are similar to those widely consumed in France.

In Labourd, oysters are eaten in a very original way—instead of being served with lemon juice, they are accompanied by a sausage called *laukenka* which has been fried beforehand.

Basque fishermen are not overly fond of oysters. However, their consumption is increasing due to the importation of excellent Galician ones.

The scallop (*Pecten jacobaeus* or *P. maximus, concha de peregrino, beira*) has almost disappeared from our coasts. I know of no other recipes than those of Galicia and France.

Freshwater mussels (gen. *Anodonta* and *Unio, almejas de río*) inhabit many Basque rivers, principally along the Mediterranean slope. They are not highly valued and are only eaten sporadically.

Sea clams (*almejas de mar, txirlak*) belong to several genera: *Tapes* (common or littleneck clam); *Donax* (wedge clam); and *Cardium* (heart cockle). It is not common to eat them raw, but they are used in soups and rice casseroles.

A very popular recipe is termed *a la marinera*. A sauce is prepared with thoroughly cleaned clams, oil, and onion, along with seasonings such as garlic, parsley, onion, cayenne pepper, *chacolí*, etc. The sauce is thickened by flour or bread crumbs.

Razor clams (*Solen marginatus, muergos, ketxos*) are not highly regarded in Zumaya, where they are used as bait for rock fishing. In Galicia they are canned and prove to be quite good. These mollusks are also called *navajas* or *mangos de cuchillo*.

CRUSTACEANS

Excellent crustacean species are found in the Basque Country, and their consumption is widespread throughout the region.

There are original recipes for certain crustaceans, but the majority of them are usually eaten after a simple cooking in salt water or in fresh water that has been salted to approximate sea water.

Barnacles

The barnacle group is very limited as to edible species. On our shores only one species, the gooseneck barnacle (*Pollicipes cornucopia, percebe, lamperna*), is eaten. It is abundant on our escarpments but is being reduced in numbers because of excessive harvesting. Gathering of this species is very dangerous, as it is undertaken during high tide near reefs and breakers.

The *lampernak* of our coasts are of the finest quality. They are cooked in salt water. Those of Fuenterrabía are well known and are an indispensable complement to the light luncheon that follows the Good Friday procession.

Shrimp, Crabs, and Lobsters

I will list the decapods that are boiled in salt water and have no special method of preparation:

- Common shrimp (*Palaemon serratus, quisquilla común* in Spanish, *iskira* in Basque)

- Grey shrimp (*Crangon crangon, camarón gris, iskira*)

- Langostino (*Nephrops norvegicus, cigala,* without a Basque name, but widely and inappropriately referred to as *langostino*)

- English lady crab or swimming crab (*Macropipus puber, nécora, txamarrak*)

- Crayfish or langostino (*Penaeus kerathurus, langostino, otarrain-txoa*)

- Green shore crab (*Carcinus maenas, cangrejo, karramarro*)

- Crab (*Cancer pagurus, cangrejo, karramarro*)

These crustaceans are usually a superb addition to fish soups.

Freshwater or estuarine shrimp (*Palaemonetes* sp.) are abundant in our rivers along the Mediterranean slope. Francisco Javier Arraiza provides a typical recipe from Ibero (Navarra). The shrimp are boiled twice and the antennae and mouth parts are removed from the head. Then they are fried in oil with a lot of garlic; finally, tomato purée is added.

The spiny lobster or langouste (*Palinurus elephas, langosta, ota-*

rraina) and the European lobster (*Homarus gammarus, bogavante, mishera*) are two crustaceans of good size and excellent meat. The quality of both is very similar, but one of those phenomena relative to questions of taste occurs—the Basque people prefer spiny lobster to European lobster and pay double for the langouste. I think that the explanation is found, as it is in many other aspects of life, in the vanity of the public. In any banquet, the appearance of European lobster could indicate miserliness on the part of the hosts. In French cooking, both species have the same status.

I can find no typical Basque recipe for lobster except one called *langosta a la Ramuntxo* which appears in the book by Ignacio Domenech. Actually, I have never seen this dish advertised in any of our restaurants, but its preparation is included in the classic line of Basque recipes.

The lobsters are divided longitudinally and placed in a casserole dish with clams. A little laurel and oregano may be added to a glass of cider. Tomato purée and a couple of finely chopped salt-cured anchovies are mixed into the cider broth, and the sauce is added to the dish. The mixture is simmered until the lobsters are well cooked.

The lobsters are then simmered slowly in a sauté of onion and ham, which should be flavored with pepper and rum; the cooking broth is added to the concoction, and this combination is then given a quick boiling. The dish is adorned with fried green peppers.

The river crayfish (*Austropotamopius pallipes, cangrejo de río, karramarro*) has always been plentiful in the Basque Country. Today, however, due to the increase in human population and industrialization, it is disappearing from our rivers.

In the slow rivers on the plains of Alava, crayfish find an ideal habitat for development. In Vitoria, it is a pleasurable experience to view the gorgeous specimens displayed for sale. It is a shame that the book by

Elvira Arias de Apraiz (a Vitorian) devotes only two lines to the preparation of crayfish.

River crayfish are generally boiled. A soup made with crayfish and rice is also prepared. In Mallavia I have eaten this soup prepared in a way similar to the *armoricana* (Breton) method.

Teodoro Bardají, in his book *La cocina de ellas,* provides the recipe for Crayfish Ataun Style. The great chef praises the quality of the crayfish caught in that Guipuzcoan village and explains the manner of preparing them. A fried mixture is made with oil, garlic, onion, *choricero* peppers, and cayenne pepper; when the onion begins to brown, the previously cleaned crayfish are added. The casserole is covered and, when the crayfish begin to change color, a glass of dry brandy is added. After this has evaporated, white wine and salt are added to the entire mixture and it is set at a slow boil.

The spider crab (*Maja squinado, centolla, txangurro*) is a good-sized crustacean of excellent meat. Its shell is usually covered with algae and marine animals that the crab has gathered with its pincers and used for camouflage.

On the Cantabrian coast the spider crab is prepared by boiling, but in our Guipuzcoan ports it is fixed in an original and excellent way. This preparation has a grand appearance because the shell itself serves as the serving receptacle. *Txangurro* prepared in this manner is on the same level as the elegant preparations of lobster.

The live crab is introduced when sea water reaches a full boil. The heat is kept high enough so that rapid boiling is maintained for fifteen or twenty minutes. In this Basque dish, the entire crab is included with the exception of the gills. All tender parts are cut up and mixed together: muscular masses, hepatopancreas (midgut gland), the digestive tract and its contents, etc.

A *mirepoix* is prepared that is flavored with sherry, Madeira, cognac, or rum; a thick tomato purée and the chopped-up crab meat are added to the mixture. This preparation can be seasoned with salt, paprika, and cayenne pepper. The shell is filled with the mixture and sprinkled with bread crumbs and chopped parsley. Pats of butter are added and it is then broiled in the oven.

In the majority of restaurants this dish is adulterated with other fish and sometimes with leftovers from previous meals. The fraudulent mixture is loaded with cayenne pepper and paprika, and this is the origin of the general belief that *txangurro* is indigestible. It is a rich and spicy dish, but not enough so to merit this slur. Seasoned within reason and without fraudulent intent it is a perfectly digestible dish.

FISH

Fish species comprise the major portion of the diet of our fishermen. I will continue to group the species in the manner we followed for mollusks and crustaceans.

Lampreys

Lampreys are the most primitive fish. They have a cartilaginous skeleton and do not have jaws, scales, swimming bladders, or pairs of fins.

The common sea lamprey (*Petromyzon marinus*) and the river lamprey (*Lampetra fluviatilis*)—both called *lamprea* in Spanish, *lampardi* or *maskar* in Basque—must have been common in earlier times in the Basque Country, but the contamination of our waters has practically exterminated them or forced them to migrate. They are fish that require extremely clear waters for reproduction. Lampreys are now so scarce that I have not had the opportunity to see them or taste them in our country. When I have had occasion to do so, it has been outside of the Basque Country.

Domenech gives two recipes for this fish: lamprey *a la donostiarra* (in the style of San Sebastián) and fishermen's lamprey. Neither formula offers much individuality other than in the main ingredient used.

Sharks and Rays

Sharks and rays have a cartilaginous skeleton and are easy to recognize in the markets—they have denticles in place of scales and their mouths are in a ventral position. They are meaty fish, although in some books the ray or skate is included among the more delicate species.

The list of these types of fish common to our markets follows:

○ Mako and requiem sharks (gen. *Isurus* and *Carcharhinus, marrajos, tintoletas*)

○ Thresher shark (*Alopias vulpinus, pez zorra, txitxi ezpata*)

○ Small-spotted catshark (*Scyliorhinus canicula, pintarrojas, katuarrain*)

○ Blackmouth catshark (*Galeus melastomus, bocanegra, pimpinua*)

○ Leafscale gulper shark or dogfish (*Centrophorus squamosus, lija, pikua*)

○ Angelshark or monkfish (*Squatina squatina, pez ángel, aingeruguardakoa*)

○ Starry smooth-hound (*Mustelus asterias, cazón, tolla*)

In a culinary sense, the best among those fish with an underdeveloped bone structure is the ray or skate (genus *Raja*) of which various species are fished and consumed. These rays and skates are known in Spanish as

raya and in Basque by the names *serra, arraizabal, aluba, ikara,* and *tramana.*

The meat of the ray is not as bad as some say nor as exquisite as others pretend. It is a nutritious fish but very inferior to the majority of the bony fishes that exist along our coasts.

Because of their considerable size, rays should always be boiled first and later prepared in whatever manner is desired. There is a recipe, highly esteemed by the French, called *raie au beurre noir* which uses a browned butter sauce.

Bony Fishes

Salmon and Trout

The aristocrats of freshwater fish belong to the trout and salmon family. It is unnecessary to eulogize here such excellent fish.

The salmon (*Salmo salar, salmón, izoki*) is an ocean fish captured in fresh water when it comes upriver to spawn. In another age, salmon must have been quite plentiful in our rivers; today they are only found in the Bidasoa and in the province of Labourd. The Bidasoa salmon is world famous, but its capture is so limited that it is rarely consumed outside the Irún area. I know of no typical Basque preparation, but it may very well be that some original recipe exists in the Bidasoa region.

The trout (*Salmo trutta* and *S. gairdneri, trucha, amuarrain*) is a fish of very delicate meat, but it is not prepared in a correct or original way. Because of the scarcity of recipes for both trout and salmon, the notion is reinforced that the Basque of the interior has less gastronomic imagination than the coastal Basque.

Trout meat is somewhat bland, and frying it in bacon or ham grease will give it flavor. This procedure is by no means to be disdained, but it

seems a little bit barbarous when applied to the delicate meat of the trout.

In some places, trout are salted for a few hours before frying. In this way, they are salted and dried at the same time.

In other cuisines distinct from our own, they are poached in aromatic broths, a practice that in my mind is more consonant with the nature of the meat. The finest procedure in this category is that of trout prepared *au bleu.*

Neither the smoking of salmon nor the pickling of trout, practices comparatively frequent in other countries, is done in the Basque Country.

Anchovies and Sardines

The anchovy (*Engraulis encrasicolus, anchoa, bokarta*), is one of the most abundant fish along our coasts and is of fundamental importance in the life of the fisherman. Anchovies are usually fished during spring, but sometimes for unknown reasons large catches are brought in throughout the year. They comprise a healthy, savory, and plentiful dish. The abundance of anchovies is in part the reason that they are not appreciated to their full value. They are usually eaten fried, but the repertory of preparation methods is extensive:

○ Anchovies floured and fried

○ Anchovies boned, floured, dipped in egg, and fried

○ Small anchovies fried in an omelet

○ Anchovies *al pil-pil*—cooked and fried in oil with garlic and red pepper

○ Anchovies *a la marinera*—cooked in oil, cider, or *chacolí* and seasoned with red pepper, parsley, and onion

O Anchovies in brine—excellent as an appetizer and in certain fish sauces

The sardine (*Sardina pilchardus, sardina*), illustrious lady of our seas in the summer months, is a flavorful fish of great nutritional value. Its presence is more irregular than that of anchovies, and for many years sardines have been very scarce.

The condition of the waters has a significant influence on the quality of the fish. Accordingly, those caught in winter are bland and meager, whereas those of midsummer are fat and delicious. It used to be said that the sardine should be eaten between Virgen del Carmen (July 16) and Assumption (August 15). This is perhaps too strictly limited, but without a doubt it is precisely in this period when they are the tastiest. Sardines are prepared in various forms:

O Sardines *a la marinera*—prepared in the same way as anchovies

O Sardines *laurak-bat* (four in one)—a recipe from Domenech that becomes a refined *marmitako* (stew) to which a purée of green peppers grilled in oil and garlic is added

O Sardines floured and fried

O Sardines boned, floured, dipped in egg, and then fried—an excellent dish for summer outdoor cooking

O Sardines with tomato sauce—the same as *a la marinera,* with the addition of tomato purée

O Sardines preserved in oil (commercially)—the canning factories shut down in periods of scarcity

○   Sardines grilled over coals

Grilling sardines over coals is the best method of preparation. It is difficult to find a fish recipe that tastes more "from the sea" than the grilled sardine.

Because this is a very greasy dish, one can tire of it on repeated dining. It is also a snack, however, and accompanied by cider makes a perfect combination.

Sardines must be grilled whole over coals that are without flames. Upon heating, the skin forms a kind of shell. Only the muscle mass is eaten. The viscera do no more than provide fat for the muscles.

Julio Camba, a great admirer of this dish, calls it *canaille* (roughly translated as "that which is vulgar"), not only for its strong flavor but also because it must be eaten with the fingers. It cannot be served on elegant tables. In Vizcaya the sardines are customarily wrapped in fig leaves.

Carps and Loaches

Fish of the carp family are abundant in our rivers. The main species are:

○   Carp (*Cyprinus carpio, carpa*)

○   Barbel (*Barbus barbus, barbo*)

○   Tench (*Tinca tinca, tenca*)

○   Nase (*Chondrostoma nasus, madrilla*)

○   Soiffe (*Chondrostoma toxostoma, loina*)

○   Spined loach (*Cobitis taenia, falsa lamprea, sarbo*)

There are no special preparations for these fish with the exception of *sarbo* which is highly esteemed in Vizcaya and the adjacent areas of Guipúzcoa. The basis of most of the preparations for these fish is garlic, parsley, and oil.

Eels

The eel family is a small but interesting group from our point of view.

The eel (*Anguilla anguilla—anguila, angira* in the adult state, and *angula, txitxardin* in the immature phase) is a most plentiful fish along our coasts and in our rivers. Until recently, its life cycle was unknown, and many legends circulated about it. Today, the mystery of its reproduction has been cleared up.

Immature eels, called elvers, constitute without a doubt one of the dishes most desired by Basques. It is one of the most original recipes in our cuisine. As I said before, there have been fabulous legends concerning these tender little fish, and even today uninformed people argue over whether or not they are actually the young of the eel.

Thanks to the studies of Schmidt, Gandolfi, and other investigators, we know in general the life cycle of the eels. The eels of our rivers begin a fall journey toward the sea when they have reached a certain stage in their development. The journey is of a nuptial nature and ends in the Sargasso Sea, where the birth of the young takes place. The newborn eels, having the shape of tiny laurel leaves, begin the arduous journey toward the rivers their parents abandoned.

This northward migration begins in the spring, and during the first summer they pass longitude 50°W. In the second summer they move toward the Azores. By now their initial size upon migrating (less than half an inch) has increased five times. During the third summer they reach our coasts and are ready to enter the rivers with the first autumn freshets. At this stage their shape is not flattened but rather cylindrical. This is the exact moment at which the culinary genius of our Basque fishermen takes over.

The eels and elvers are plentiful in all of Europe, with the exception of the Black Sea and its tributary rivers. Yet I believe that only in our country have people dared to prepare and consume a dish which resembles a bunch of worms. Eels have very tasty meat. They are more highly appreciated by the Basques of the Ebro basin than by the Cantabrian Basques.

Elvers constitute a very complete meal—it should be noted that the animal is eaten whole—with an agreeable physical sensation to the palate and a very mild taste. This flavor is easily perceived and quite agreeable in boiled elvers, but in the common form of preparation—*al pil-pil*—the unique taste is significantly masked by garlic, oil, and hot red pepper. In order that elvers be agreeable to the palate, they must be prepared with utmost care, and strict rules of procedure must be followed.

Elvers must be alive and then must be killed quickly. To accomplish this they are dropped in water made strongly nicotinic (by the addition of tobacco). Once dead, they are carefully cleaned until the abundant mucus which covers them is removed. This removal of mucus is essential, because upon cooking, the mucus would congeal into clots, resulting in a significant loss to the overall quality of the dish.

Once properly cleaned, they are "coagulated" in salted water at a full boil. The word "coagulate" is used because elvers are like transparent gelatin. In a few minutes, through the action of the heat, they are converted into the white or black-white animals known throughout the world. Gradations in whiteness are due to a simple increase in pigmentation as the elvers proceed upstream through the rivers.

Elvers are generally sold in the markets in this cleaned and cooked

state. In the last phase of preparation, they are first submerged in salty, tepid water for a final cleansing. They are then placed on clean cloths to be drained of excess water but at the same time kept moist.

Olive oil of the finest quality is placed in a *cazuela* (clay casserole) and pieces of garlic are browned in it. The casserole is then taken off the heat. Finely chopped red pepper is added, and when the oil has lowered in temperature the elvers are added.

The clay casserole is immediately placed on the fire. The elvers cannot begin to fry yet, because the abundant liquid that the elvers emit must first evaporate. Soon a subtle, pleasant crackling begins, and when the bubbling has spread throughout the casserole the dish is ready to be served.

The *cazuela* in which the elvers are traditionally prepared and served is made of fired clay. As was mentioned earlier, this casserole retains heat better than one made of iron.

There is a difference among the various eel catches. Inhabitants along the various rivers engage in great discussions concerning the quality of elvers captured in different areas. The eels that enter our rivers are without a doubt all of a common origin and were comparable before the Basque Country was industrialized. Today each river has its own specific refuse, and perhaps as a result, the different eel populations may vary in quality.

For me, the true difference is due to distinct methods of preparation. The young eel is such a delicate organism that it cannot be handled in great quantities without harm. Success lies in not heaping them up and overcooking them, events which occur too easily when there is an excess of handling in the process.

There is an extravagant Basque recipe for hake, called *medallones de merluza euskal etxea,* in which elvers serve as a side dish. Normally, however, every Basque considers it culinary heresy to eat elvers in any way other than *al pil-pil.*

Adult eels are prepared in *salsa verde* and constitute an exquisite dish in the season of peas, asparagus, and artichokes. In the Ribera de Navarra region they are eaten with immature beans (*pochas*) and are also prepared with tomato and pepper. Eel blood contains a toxic substance called ichthyotoxin. This blood is often given mixed with wine to alcoholics to aid in their cure. It loses its toxicity through the action of heat.

The conger eel (*Conger conger, congrio, itxar*) is plentiful on our coasts and in our markets. Its meat is good, but half of its bulk is full of spines. This proves considerably inconvenient for serving it in slices. It can be used in the making of soup. Conger eel in *salsa verde* is excellent. Long ago it was eaten much more frequently.

Mullets

Mullets inhabit our rivers but are not generally valued. The striped mullet (*Mugil cephalus*) and the golden grey mullet (*Liza aurata*) share the same common names in Spanish (*mujol, lisa*) and in Basque (*korkon*).

Very plentiful in our rivers and river mouths, these fish find the greater part of their own nourishment in the mud and waste of sewers and backwaters. Those that live in clean areas or among the rocks have very fine meat and are highly valued along the coast. They are virtually unknown in the kitchens of the interior.

Domenech has a recipe, *corcones al chacolí,* that must be excellent, although I do not believe it is widespread. I say this because sorrel is used

in this dish, and although it grows wild in our land, this plant is not eaten except on rare occasions.

Needlefishes

The needlefish group is limited in species as well as in gastronomic qualities. The garfish (*Belone belone, aguja, akula*) belongs to this family but is not esteemed on the coast. Along the Mediterranean slope it is highly sought for its strong taste. It is also called beaked sardine in this area.

Garfish is widely used as a counterfeit for anchovies in brine. Preserved in oil in the style of canned sardines, it is quite acceptable.

Alfonsinos

We only eat one variety of the alfonsino family. The beryx (*Beryx decadactylus*)—*besugo* or *cachucho* in Spanish and *bixigu-errea* in Basque—is a wonderful fish of rosy color, ample size, enormous eyes, and a savory and delicate meat.

Sea Basses and Croakers

Sea basses and croakers are great fish as regards genealogy, appearance, and quality.

Heading the group is the coveted sea bass (*Dicentrarchus labrax, lubina, lupia*), a marvelous fish found just off the steep cliffs of our coast. Its white meat, delicate and firm, is delicious to the most demanding of palates.

The great monster of this family is the red grouper (*mero*). Lafitte mentions two types: the wreckfish or stone bass (*Polyprion americanus, roca*), and the grouper or dusky perch (*Epinephelus guaza, mero de altura, kraba*).

Red grouper has a firm and tough meat and it keeps much better after capture than the majority of fish. Its consistency allows it to be grilled over a fire as if it were beef.

The comber (*Serranus cabrilla, cabrilla, kraba*) is of fine meat and is eaten fried or boiled.

The croaker or corvina (*Umbrina cirrosa, corvina, gurbi*), and its near relative the meagre (*Sciaena aquila, antesa*) are fished off of the rocks.

Apart from red grouper, it is uncommon to find fish of this group in the markets, given that they are generally consumed in the same areas in which they are fished. I know of no typical form of preparation in the Basque Country. In the book *El Amparo* two recipes are given but lack any specific information about the corvina. In the book by the Marquesa de Parabere there are some sea bass recipes.

Red grouper is usually cooked in a good broth, in the oven, or on the grill. The sea bass and the corvina adapt as well to roasting and grilling as to boiling. The sea bass is beyond a doubt one of the best fish of our seas.

Sea-breams

The sea-bream group provides us with some of our most esteemed fish.

The red sea-bream (*Pagellus bogaraveo, besugo* or *errosel, bixigua*) is a well-known and popular fish. Some have said that the name *besugo* is of Basque origin but the truth remains uncertain.

It has been an extremely well known fish for ages—the fourteenth-century Archpriest of Hita referred to it. Sea-bream is our classic winter fish, and no Christmas dinner is complete without it. It reaches optimum quality in December and January.

The sea-bream allows for all methods of culinary preparation—boiling, frying, baking, stewing, and pickling—but it tastes best when grilled over coals.

This method of roasting over the coals requires considerable practice to achieve the precise cooking conditions necessary. Antonio Peña y Goñi, at the end of the nineteenth century, described the roasting of sea-bream in San Sebastián in this way:

> The sea-bream is cleaned with much care. It is salted and left to dry in a fresh and convenient place. An hour before serving the fish is placed on a grill under which a live fire of holm oak charcoal burns. Take the feather of a capon, moisten well with good, unrefined oil and lightly oil the sea-bream, turning it until the skin is well grilled. Just before serving, singe the fish in very hot oil with garlic and a little lemon.

These basic and primitive grilling recipes have never been improved upon through new formulas or innovative techniques.

Nothing can surpass a well-cooked, magnificent sea-bream on a cold December day. After having assuaged our palates with a plate of fine cabbage, we are brought a succulent sea-bream, its white meat dotted with bits of red pepper and garlic cloves. At such a moment it is inconceivable that any other dish could substitute for the fish which we now have before us.

The young offspring of the red sea-bream (*P. bogaraveo, pancho, albano*) are of small size and quite plentiful inshore along the wharves. The meat is delicate but the preponderance of spines impedes its consumption.

The pandora (*Pagellus erythrinus, breca, lamote*) is a first cousin of the red sea-bream, but of a rosier appearance and without the black mark at the base of the lateral line.

The gilthead (*Sparus aurata, dorada, urraburu*) is a magnificent fish that bears a sign of its nobility in the frontal region and has a fierce, "armored" mouth. For many gourmets it is the finest among rock fish. The back of the neck of a roasted gilthead is an exceptional dish.

The porgy or common sea-bream (*Pagrus pagrus, pargo, urta* or *txelba*), the blacksmith fish (*Pagellus mormyrus, pez herrera, erla*), the sargo (*Diplodus sargus, sargo, musharra*), and the oblada (*Oblada melanura, oblada, buztanbeltza*) are other excellent representatives of this group but are not well known beyond this coast.

Wrasses

There are few varieties of wrasses, and they are of little importance as food sources. For Lozano Rey the cuckoo wrasse (*Labrus mixtus, maragota*) is the *durdo*, whereas for Laffitte the ballan wrasse (*Labrus bergylta, bodión*) is the Basque *durdo* and the *maragota* is our *txilibitu*. The rainbow wrasse (*Coris julis, julia, doncella*) is not widely eaten.

Goatfishes

The only goatfishes (also called red mullets) used for food are from the genus *Mullus*. Two species are both named *barbarina* in Basque: the red mullet (*Mullus surmuletus, salmonete de roca*), striped and with a long snout; and the mud mullet (*Mullus barbatus, salmonete de fango*). The first is of better quality than the second.

Mackerel and Tuna

The mackerel family is of enormous economic importance due to the fact that within it are found very delectable fish caught in great quantities.

The Atlantic mackerel (*Scomber scombrus, verdel, berdela*) has a fatty meat and is very pleasant when either fried or roasted.

The blue-fin tuna (*Thunnus thynnus, atún, egalabur* or *cima-rroya*) is very large. Its red meat, fatty and firm, is not as highly valued as that of other species of the group, despite the fact that it is very nutritious. It is sometimes referred to as "tuna for the masses."

Under the name *bonito* three species of this group are confused: the albacore (*Thunnus alalunga, albácora, egaluze*), the true Atlantic bonito (*Sarda sarda, bonito*), and the *lampo* of whose technical name I am unsure.

Thousands of tons of these fish are harvested all year long, although each species has specific seasons in which the largest captures are made. Tuna is not only the staple of fishermen throughout various months but also the prime material for the numerous and important canning factories established along our coasts.

Tuna stew (*marmitako*) is a very typical dish. The ventral section of the tuna, called *ventrecha* or *mendreska,* is delicious when grilled. This section contains the musculature generously laced with fat which makes the dish slightly indigestible, but it is no less succulent than the other parts of the fish.

Tuna is cooked by all methods—grilled, baked, and fried—and is exceptional when fried with tomato, onion, and pepper.

Scad

The scad or horse mackerel (*Trachurus trachurus, chicharro*) is what we might call "poor man's sea-bream," because the large catches coincide with those of the sea-bream and because it is much more rea-

sonable in price. It is popular among the general public at the end of autumn and in the winter.

It is an excellent dish and when grilled constitutes a very complete meal. Its meat is somewhat darker than that of sea-bream and so is lower in price.

Scorpionfishes (Rockfishes)

Scorpion fish (*Scorpaena porcus* and *S. scrofa, cabracho, kabrarroka*) are excellent fish of white and flavorful meat. These fish form excellent meals when boiled, grilled, or baked. Their meat should be included in all good fish soups.

The spines are covered by a toxic mucus that makes wounds inflicted by them quite painful.

Searobins or Gurnards

Several gurnards have white meat, and the following species are called *rubios* in Spanish and *arraigorriak* in Basque: the piper (*Trigla lyra*), the red gurnard (*Aspitrigla cuculus*), the streaked gurnard (*Trigloporus lastoviza*), and the tub gurnard (*Trigla lucerna*). These fish are considerably esteemed and are excellent when boiled or when added to soup.

Soles and Flounders

All the members of the flatfish group are strangely shaped, but their appearance does not affect the excellent quality of many varieties.

Sole (*Solea solea, lenguado, lenguana*) is prepared in a wide variety of ways in many countries, and it is one of the most valued fish. For some unknown reason, sole caught off of our coasts is not treated in any special manner, and Basques settle for frying it when not attempting to copy more exotic methods.

The dab (*Limanda limanda, gallo, oilar*) is a good fish, although it is not as firm as sole. When filleted, it usually passes for sole in many restaurants. It is easy to distinguish between them, but the high cost of sole is the reason many people are not overly familiar with it.

The turbot (*Scophthalmus maximus, rodaballo, errebollua*) is a magnificent representative of this group. Although it may be prepared in many ways, it is best in *salsa verde*. It is the fish which produces the thickest sauce when fixed in this manner. In spring, accompanied by peas, asparagus, and fresh artichokes, turbot is an exceptional dish.

Poor relatives of this family are the plaice (*Pleuronectes platessa*) and flounder (*Platichthys flesus*), both called *platija* in Spanish and *platusa* in Basque. They have ample meat and are common in the markets.

Weevers

The greater weever (*Trachinus draco*) and lesser weever (*Echiichthys vipera*)—both called *pez araña* in Spanish, *xabiron* and *salbera* in Basque—are excellent fish of firm meat. They can be very dangerous while alive due to highly venomous spines which can cause extremely painful wounds. The venom loses its toxicity when heated, but extraordinary care must be taken in handling the fresh fish.

Cod and Hake

Hake and cod are very important fish. We will dedicate separate sections to these two species.

Cod. The cod most frequently eaten today is *Gadus morhua* (*baca-*

lao, makailo), which has been gutted and cured before it reaches our markets. This species does not inhabit our coasts. Those fish called fresh cod in the markets are specimens of whiting (*Merlangius merlangus*) or pollack (*Pollachius pollachius*).

The true codfish or *bacalao* inhabits the North Atlantic, spreading throughout the European area from France to Norway. Its appearance in Cantabrian waters is rare. It prefers the deep waters of cold seas.

According to some, the term *bacalao,* as well as the Danish word *bakelau* and the Dutch *baukaelja,* is derived from the island of Bacalieu, near Newfoundland. According to others, *bacalao* comes from the Gaelic word *bachall,* a type of pole on which *bacalao* was once dried.

Whatever the etymology of the word, the fact remains that cod is of great economic importance and for centuries has played a vital role in the nutrition of European peoples. Arguments over cod and whales have spurred on numerous wars and disputes, and through the centuries diplomats have had to negotiate these constant disagreements between the fishermen of different nationalities.

Up until recently, cod was caught by hook only and prepared and cured on shore near its native waters. Today it is widely fished with nets and prepared in commercial factories.

The same thing has happened with cod as with chorizos, hams, wines, liquors, etc. Industry has ensured uniformity and economy in these products, but the quality of the more naturally prepared foodstuffs cannot be maintained. In industrial preparation of cod, heat, cold, and chemicals enter into the process. The economic results are favorable but the gastronomic ones are detestable. A well-cured *bacalao* should ideally possess white and flexible meat, dark skin, and its own unique smell which it should maintain throughout culinary preparation.

Basque fishermen have caught and consumed this fish for centuries.

Today cod is considered second-rate in the majority of countries, but in our country it is prepared with a particular technique that raises its status and converts it into a dish worthy of the finest tables.

The culinary problem of converting a dried and cured fish into a succulent dish has been solved by following either of two completely different procedures.

One method—primitive and rough—is the one used in the preparation of *zurrukutuna* and *ajo arriero*. In this procedure pieces of cured cod are grilled over coals. Aided by the heat, the salt impregnates the fish and removes the little water that remains in the cells. At that moment, the pieces dampen and go soft. In this state it is easy to remove the skin and spines and at the same time break the white meat sections into pieces. The fish is rinsed with water to remove excess salt. In this way it is readied for its final preparation.

To make *ajo arriero,* the cod is soaked in an oil in which generous amounts of chopped garlic, peeled peppers, tomatoes, and red peppers have been browned. This original dish is very different from the effeminate *ajo arriero* that is served in many restaurants, where the dish is not only robbed of its flavor but also adulterated with lobster.

In the countryside, *ajo arriero*—accompanied by a wine of the quality of a Murchante and a good bread made with flour from the Bardenas—is a good culinary representative of the noble Ribera region and is a delight to the palate.

Zurrukutuna begins with the same desalting process used for *ajo arriero,* and the cod is then added to a soup along with tomato and bread. There are many recipes, all more refined than that for *ajo arriero.*

The second preparation of *bacalao* is slow, smooth, and wise. Created on the coast, it is one of the glories of Basque cooking. The cod undergoes a two-part preparation: the desalting and then the tempering

or setting of the *bacalao* in hot water. The best procedure for desalting is to submerge the fish in a river or stream of clean water for about eighteen hours.

When our rivers deserved the name "river" and were not full of contaminants and sewage as they are today, they well could have accommodated such an operation. Now we must settle for immersing the fish in large vessels of cold water and changing the water every four or five hours.

After this time spent in the water, the cells—now salt-free—are in a condition to recover a lot of the water lost in the curing process.

To temper the cod, the pieces are placed in a pot with cold water and put on the heat in such a way that the temperature rises slowly. The temperature of the water should not exceed 65° C (150° F). The operation of tempering is the criterion for knowing the quality of the fish. If it is of prime quality it will become white, firm, and smooth. If it is a commercial *bacalao* in which chemicals have been introduced, we will end up with a fibrous mass, and in this case it is best not to continue with the preparation. Cod can be in the water at 60° C (140° F) for about forty-five to sixty minutes.

There is a method for rapid tempering which consists of heating the pot as rapidly as possible until a froth appears on the surface. This operation must be carefully watched. It is justified only as a time-saving measure, because if the water reaches 90° C (195° F) the precious gelatins in the skin are lost.

Now the *bacalao* is ready for the final stage of preparation. We will review the method called *a la vizcaina* first, given its excellence and popularity. This sauce essentially consists of a purée of onions and *choricero* peppers, using lard and bacon grease as fat. In general, all red sauces are referred to as *a la vizcaina,* but this a gross error. After consulting various books and recipes I remain convinced—despite the objections of others—that in the sauce properly called *a la vizcaina,* the only red element should be that of the *choricero* pepper, not tomatoes or sweet peppers. The recipe of the old Bilbao restaurant El Amparo, in my opinion, is not only the most genuine and authentic but also the best.

The El Amparo preparation begins with onions (not sweet) that are chopped and slowly cooked in a casserole with lard. The addition of olive oil is not obligatory. A little parsley, ham, and black pepper may be added. The procedure must be gradual so that any small amount of sugar in the onion does not become caramelized.

After about three hours the mass is considerably reduced, boiling water is added, and it continues to boil for two more hours. It is then strained through a fine colander, and the pulp of *choriceros*—one pepper per slice of fish—is added. (Prior to their addition, the *choriceros* are soaked in water for about twelve hours.) Two hard-cooked egg yolks are mixed with water and a little bacon grease and then added to the mixture. The fish slices are placed in a clay casserole skin side up, without stacking; the purée is added, and the dish is set to simmer slowly until the ingredients become well integrated.

The dish improves upon this slow reheating. It seems as if, in the time lapse between preparation and reheating, the flavors of the sauce and the fish are intensified. With fresh fish the interchange of flavors is quick, but it seems as if the cells of the cured cod are a bit inert due to the tempering process.

There are at least three other great recipes in which tempered cod is used. These authentic Basque preparations are briefly described below.

Cod *al pil-pil* is boiled down by putting slices of fish in the finest olive oil and giving them a treatment similar to that used on young eels. The oil should remain transparent. Because of the simplicity of this method, the fish must be of the highest quality. There exists no sauce which can cover up any inherent defects.

Bacalao ligado, frequently confused with *bacalao al pil-pil,* is made with a sauce that is similar to that of *salsa verde,* which we mention in the section on hake. In the case of cod, some of water in which the fish has been soaked is added to the dish because the slices of cod do not contain enough water to produce an emulsion despite prolonged soaking.

The third and, for me, the finest method for preparing cod is *bacalao al Club Ranero.* This recipe is very well described in the *Enciclopedia culinaria.* It is a *bacalao ligado* to which is added a fried mixture of green peppers, onions, and tomatoes. The mixture is fried well, but care is taken that the elements do not fall apart. The recipe is a creation of the French chef Caveriviere and, although it is not well known and of foreign origin, I have included it in the recipe section, considering it to be the finest way of preparing cod in the Basque manner.

Hake. The hake (*Merluccius merluccius, merluza, legatza*) is a fundamental fish in Basque cooking. It is still caught by hook in some ports and, fished in this manner, its quality is optimum. The majority of hake in the markets, however, are caught by net.

Hake meat is fine, white, nutritious, quite digestible, and allows for varied handling. It is eaten whole, and even its gular (throat) region is dissected to extract the delicious *kokotxak* ("cheeks"), a true delicacy.

Merluza en salsa verde involves all parts of the fish; even the head and the area right behind it admirably enhance this preparation. The *salsa verde* is an emulsion of oil and the juices from the hake. It is produced in the presence of garlic and seasoned with parsley.

The hake is placed in oil in which chopped garlic has been partially

fried. The dish is placed on low heat, which causes the fish to emit a good deal of liquid. While this is flowing out, it mixes with the oil through the emulsifying action of the garlic. The operation is aided by gentle movement of the casserole or skillet. A real emulsion is then formed—a mixture which, according to Professor Dastre of the Sorbonne, becomes a perfect ménage à trois with the addition of parsley. The dish we are considering is in fact a "ménage à quatre" given that the hake, not part of the actual sauce, is necessary to furnish the aqueous juices. There are many variations of this sauce. The recipe just outlined is the simplest and, by my standards, the best.

Hake must be dehydrated to some extent before preparation to avoid the possibility of its emitting too much juice. Dehydration is done by salting the fish and setting it aside for a couple of hours.

The widely popularized fried hake is achieved by flouring the slices of fish, dipping them in beaten egg, and frying them in oil which is not too hot. In this way an almost impermeable cap is formed which impedes drying, and the fish is therefore juicy and delicious. The southern peoples of the Basque Country fry their fish without coating them first and at high temperature.

Hake is prepared in many other ways—baked, boiled, stewed in different styles—but the two methods described above are to my understanding the best and most classic.

Basque people highly value hake; proof of that fact is in the prices it commands, even though it is a plentiful fish all year long.

Anglerfishes

We conclude this lengthy chapter on seafood with the anglerfish group. Its only representative is the angler (*Lophius piscatorius, rape, sapua*). It is fitting that the last fish to become popularized among the

Basques closes this section. The angler was esteemed in some ports, but otherwise it was almost unknown until 1936. Catalonian refugees taught the Guipuzcoans of the interior regions, and many of the coastal areas, to eat angler.

It is a fish that expels a good deal of liquid when cooked, so it is necessary to dehydrate it first. Once boiled, baked, or stewed, it has a firm, white meat which is very flavorful and reminds one of shellfish. I say "reminds" and not "is similar." It seems as if angler passes for lobster in many restaurants. I think such a blatant mistake could only happen among those who are not familiar with that crustacean.

METHODS OF FISH AND SEAFOOD PREPARATION

In general, the fish found in our markets are excellent, but I think it opportune to give a few practical rules to aid in a quick determination of quality. Fresh fish must have the following characteristics:

○ The skin should be glistening and iridescent, with tinges of vital color. The fish that loses these characteristics a few hours after capture continues to be good for a short while, but must still show at least some vital coloring.

○ The scales must be firmly attached. There are a few exceptions such as sardines and anchovies.

○ The meat should be rigid, firm, and consistent. It should give the sensation of "live" meat upon touching. Fish caught in a net, although they are fresh, do not usually possess this characteristic.

○ The stomach should not be distended. The anal orifice should be closed.

○ The fins should be whole, well attached, and resistant to pulling.

○ The eyes should be clear and transparent, filling the eyeball socket. The cornea should be convex, with the blood vessels clearly visible.

○ The gills should be red, shiny, and without mucus. A lessening in color is allowable, but not in the shine. To fool the buyer, the gills are sometimes painted with blood.

○ The smell must be agreeable, never ammonia-like. The ray or skate is an exception in that its external mucus deteriorates rapidly, giving it an ammonia smell.

Almost all of these tips come from *El libro del pescado,* by Imanol Beleak.

In general, the Basque fishermen do not eat fish right after their capture. Here, it is not common to bring fish to the frying pan "alive and swimming." When the fish reaches the kitchen it is immediately disemboweled. It is cleaned, salted, and left to sit a few hours. Through the action of the salt and air the fish is slightly dehydrated. The meat stays firm and smooth and does not leak too much fluid.

Types of Preparation

Raw. Only mollusks such as oysters and clams are eaten raw. They are usually accompanied by lemon juice. In Labourd, oysters are usually eaten with sausages called *laukenkak.* I know of no recipe for raw fish in Basque cooking.

Cured. Much cured and salted fish is eaten. Codfish is the species most often prepared in this manner. Squid and various other species are sometimes prepared in this way.

Boiled. Much boiled fish is eaten, although the Basque fisherman does not often use the broths of French cuisine. (The so-called *caldo corto* is nothing more than a poor interpretation of the French *court-bouillon.*)

The liquid for cooking is usually just salted water. Afterward, the fish is simmered in a mixture of oil, garlic, and red pepper. The most well known preparation of this kind is Eels *al pil-pil.*

Fried. Olive oil is generally used for frying. In contrast with the Andalucians, we use a relatively small quantity of oil at low temperature.

Medium- and large-sized fish cannot be fried effectively, even when care is taken, because the exterior becomes burned while the interior remains uncooked. For this reason many fish are filleted.

To obtain good fried fish, the presence of carbohydrates is necessary. As these elements are scarce in fish, it is generally covered with flour or a batter. In Basque cooking, fish is dipped in flour and then in beaten egg. Through the action of the heat, these products form a cover which prevents the fish from drying out.

Roasted. As it is with meats, the roasting of fish is the noblest of preparations. The method is exceptional not only for its antiquity, but also because of its excellent results when correctly carried out. The best heat for roasting is that which is produced by wood coals.

Sauces. Many fish are prepared with sauces—some original, others of universal domain, and still others copied from other cuisines. The original sauces included in this book are described in conjunction with the fish for which each one is most often prepared; accordingly, the *salsa verde* (green sauce) appears under hake and Vizcayan sauce under codfish.

Fish Soups, *Tioros,* and *Marmitakos*

Preparations of seafood soups (characteristically made of boiled fish eaten in its own broth, along with bread or potatoes) are a basic nutritional element in the diet of our fishermen. The soups are usually seasoned with various agricultural products: garlic, onion, tomato, paprika, laurel, pepper, white wine, cider, etc.

The great chef and learned gourmet Teodoro Bardají begins his book *La cocina de ellas* with a maxim worthy of mention:

> Seven virtues has soup:
> It calms thirst and diminishes hunger,
> Aids in sleeping and digestion,
> Tastes good and never offends,
> And brings color to the face.

Our fishermen, taking advantage of a plentiful and varied selecton of fish and the availability of excellent garden products, prepare dishes which are more or less like stews and which play a similar role to that of the *cocidos* made in the interior zones.

The preparation of fish stock is more rapid and simpler than that of meat stock. Fish is easily broken down by boiling water, and it quickly flavors the surrounding liquid. In only a few minutes of cooking, fish becomes quite tender and is ready to be included in the soup or served as a separate dish.

The special taste of each seafood soup is due primarily to the particular variety of fish involved in its cooking. Differences in flavors can also result from the treatment of the fish; sometimes it is fried before being added to the soup. Spices also contribute to the variations.

All along the Basque coast, excellent soups of this kind are eaten. The carbohydrates included in these soups usually come from the addition of bread and, in some cases, rice.

Very often we come across soups made with a seafood species that is considered ordinary, but which is at the same time delicious. Such is the case with octopus or barnacle soup. Clam soup and soup prepared with rockfish are also very fine.

In reality these soups are very similar to those of other coasts. Only in particular cases do the great variety and quality of the Cantabrian fish contribute to dishes that prove superior to the preparations of other areas.

A relatively complicated procedure is involved in the cooking of the *tioro,* a dish of Labourdin fishermen. There are several variations, but an excellent one is included in the recipe section.

Engaged in their fishing labors, the *arrantzaleak* (Basque fishermen) prepare a dish that is nutritionally complete, tasty, and easy to prepare. This is the so-called *marmitako,* without a doubt named for the receptacle in which it has traditionally been prepared.

At present, the potato is typically the source of carbohydrates in this dish. In that this tuber is of recent introduction to our kitchens, it is presumed that bread formerly provided the carbohydrates.

The classic *marmitako* is made of tuna, but it can also be made with other fatty fish.

The recipe for this dish is given by the Bilbao intellectual, D. Pedro de Eguillor, in a piece dedicated to the Marquesa de Parabere. It appears on the first page of her book, the magnificent *Enciclopedia culinaria,* as follows:

The tuna fleet slices the sea
The hook hidden in the bait,
is tossed to the covetous fish who waits.
Caught, a victim now—his fury lost.
Meanwhile, the mate pours the oil
in the pot over the red coals boil;
Onions of their skins well-peeled
chopped fine with ease, his skill revealed.
A bonito, its flesh palpitating
is cut in little pieces, fried while waiting
in firm tomato and red pepper spicy;
Then, with water boiling, diluted quite nicely,
is left at a steady boil to entice
as the white victual weds with the spice.
And arriving at that time
when the day's labors decline,
the pot fills up to entice,
with potatoes cleaned and sliced.
When they become tender and done,
When one's energy is failing one
from that arduous labor, the sailor
at a jovial sign from the cook,
his neighbor below, sets down to devour
this dish, the *marmitako*.

The only defect in this recipe is that it truly proves difficult to cause the oil to boil *so la brasa roja*—over red coals. Otherwise, this literary composition is as delectable as the culinary one.

5

EGGS, DESSERTS, DAIRY PRODUCTS, AND BEVERAGES

EGGS, milk, cheeses, fruits, and wines and other beverages are important in the Basque kitchen. Eggs and milk are used in basic cooking (as they are in other cuisines), but this section will emphasize unique ways in which they are used in Basque cooking.

EGGS

Many animals produce eggs from which their young are born. Their nests are generally easy to find, and the eggs of many species have constituted a much sought-after food since early times. Today great quantities of chicken and duck eggs are eaten, but we should not forget that caviar, delicious and very expensive, is actually composed of the eggs of sturgeon. With other fish eggs, dishes which are relatively tasty are also prepared. Reptile eggs, such as those of the turtle, are sought by inhabitants of those areas where these animals are found. However, chicken and duck eggs, and mainly the former, are those that commonly enter into our diet.

Eggs lend themselves to quite varied concoctions that are based upon the following methods of preparation:

○ Raw

○ *À la coque*—boiled in water for three minutes

○ Soft-boiled (*mollet*)—cooked for about six minutes

○ Hard-boiled—ten to twelve minutes of boiling time

○ Poached—cooked after being shelled and without allowing the yolk to harden

○ Molded—shelled and placed in molds which are then put in a dish half-filled with warm water and cooked for six to eight minutes

○ Fried whole in oil

○ Beaten and scrambled in a little fat

○ Beaten and prepared as an omelet—well cooked but without becoming hard, and then folded

○ *Al plato* (shirred)—prepared in the oven in a greased container without letting the yolk harden

○   Roasted in hot coals

In addition to these recipes, there are various dishes—mainly desserts and sauces—in which eggs are an important ingredient.

Among Basques the use of eggs in cooking is somewhat limited. I will summarize those recipes which are considered to be Basque in origin, although they are similar to dishes in other cuisines and cultures.

In the Cantabrian area, one can find some eggs of extraordinary, almost singular quality. I believe this fact is attributable to three factors: the rarity of the high-quality eggs is due to the fact that the breeds of poultry used are unfortunately on the road to extinction; animal feed is plentiful—these chickens are not enclosed and run free to forage all day through fields and woods; and corn is an abundant element in their diet. Corn is not used, I believe, in the diets of the large poultry farms because it reduces the number of eggs laid.

Eggs al koskol. Eggs *al koskol* are cooked beneath hot coals. This is an outdated cooking method, but when fireplaces were numerous, eggs were frequently prepared in this manner. An egg cooked *al koskol* acquires a special taste that results from the albumin burning in spots where the coals touch the egg.

Piperrada (Basque omelet). Piperrada is our most famous egg recipe. Its spread to other countries has been accomplished by means of Basque restaurants along the Labourdin coastline.

Variations exist, but an excellent method consists of roasting the green *cristal* peppers, peeling and then cutting them into strips, and frying them in olive oil on low heat. Other ingredients are included and then beaten eggs are added and made into an omelet. Care is taken so that the mixture remains soft.

Mushroom omelet. The mushroom omelet is greatly appreciated in

the peninsular Basque Country.

Bayonne omelet. This soft omelet of mushrooms and Bayonne ham is covered with a little béarnaise sauce.

Pisto bilbaino. This omelet is made with ham, squash, onion, green pepper, and tomato. The vegetables and the ham are cooked slowly in oil and then combined with beaten eggs.

Fried eggs. Fried eggs are the most popular form of preparation, but for the sake of truth I would have to say that they are prepared well in few Basque kitchens. It seems that they are fried in too little oil and at too low a temperature. They are usually accompanied by potatoes, peppers, tomato, chorizo, and ham or bacon.

Frikatza. Frikatza is an egg omelet made with lamb's blood and cooked, chopped intestines. The blood is coagulated and immediately fried with the intestines. The mixture is then added to beaten eggs and the omelet is prepared.

Béarnaise sauce. Although there are many arguments about the origin of béarnaise sauce, I cannot neglect mentioning it. It is made with egg yolks, vinegar, white wine, tarragon, shallots, and butter. The emulsion should be made at a temperature between 45° C (113° F), the melting point of butter, and 65° C (150° F), the point at which egg yolk coagulates.

DESSERTS

The foods that I will now discuss make up our desserts—dishes that conclude a meal.

Fruit

Keeping in mind what I have already said about the Basque climate and soil, it is not surprising that so many varieties of fruits exist in that temperate climate and are of excellent quality.

From the lemons and oranges of the coasts to the wild raspberries of the Pyrenees, all kinds of fruits are grown on our land.

In the Cantabrian area, fruit orchards and strawberry fields grow in all their splendor. Strawberries grow wild in the mountains and are the only fruits in which the cultivated ones are not better than the wild ones. At the beginning of summer, large quantities of these small, wild strawberries are found in the markets of Pamplona.

Pears and apples, when well cultivated—an unfortunately infrequent occurrence—are usually of magnificent taste and appearance. In this Cantabrian zone, some varieties of peaches (*muxurkak*) and some types of plums are raised with great difficulty.

In the areas of the Mediterranean slope, apricot, peach, and plum trees flourish during the hot summer and fall seasons. They produce fruits of high quality which are often exported to other countries.

It is common to bake pears and apples, and apples are still roasted beneath hot coals. They form a superb winter dessert. Fruit compotes—mixtures of fruits cooked in wine, sugar, and cinnamon—are very popular. A *zurrakapote* is a compote to which dried fruits have been added—an improvement upon the basic fruit compote.

Walnut pudding (*intxaursalsa*) is made with chopped walnuts cooked in milk with sugar and cinnamon—an excellent winter dessert. Chestnuts continue to be a very popular winter dessert. They are eaten boiled or roasted in a metal utensil called a *tamboril* (*tamboliña*). I know of no preserves with a chestnut base, although in some places capons are stuffed with chestnuts. The French *marrons glacés* (chestnuts that are preserved and then glazed) are barely even known in the Basque Country.

Sweets

The repertory of sweet desserts is not very extensive in Basque cooking. The preparation of sweets, except in some cities such as Vitoria, has come upon hard times. This may be due to growing industrialization as well as little demand on the part of the public. With the exception of a few establishments, it is difficult to acquire good pastries and confections. The sweets of Labourd are worth mentioning, however, as they are pastries of the highest quality. At the same time, sweets are the least important part of the meal in Labourdian restaurants.

Without a doubt because of tradition, Vitoria has a magnificent pastry industry. In Vergara we find the famous *rellenos* (cream pastries), although there are establishments that sell poor imitations. In Segura, a delicious almond cake is prepared. Tolosa has some excellent little pastries made of almond and egg yolk. Tudela produces its famous *mantecadas* (sweet buns). There are some other towns with local specialties as well. In fact, our list is short when one considers that there are many *errikosemeak* (village sons) who would say the local sweets are of exceptional quality.

I cannot conclude this section without mentioning the extraordinary development of the chocolate industry in our country. There are numerous and important chocolate factories here. It is probable that this industry is a vestige of the past splendor of the firm known as Real Compañía Guipuzcoana de Caracas.

Abundant honey is produced, but we are not overly fond of it. The desserts that follow are the most common preparations with a sugar base.

Arroz con leche (rice pudding). There are convents and restaurants who specialize in the preparation of rice pudding, a very popular dessert. Basically, it consists of rice cooked in milk, cinnamon, and sugar.

Torradas de pan (French toast). To make French toast, bread is soaked in milk with sugar and cinnamon. The pieces are then dipped in egg and fried in pork lard.

Bizcochos de Mendaro (sponge cakes). Bizcochos are a speciality of this Guipuzcoan town. Cakes, served in small portions on paper, are covered with a white glaze of syrup and beaten egg whites.

Rellenos de Vergara (cream cakes). This cream cake, which is filled with egg cream and dipped in a syrup glaze, is quite rich. It is an excellent pastry. Poor substitutions are frequently offered, even in Vergara itself, making it difficult to find those of top quality.

My friend Josu Oregui, from Vergara, tells me it appears that the introduction of these filled cakes in Vergara was due to the festivals organized in honor of Saint Martin. Many chefs and pastry cooks must have attended, and it was one of them who left behind the recipe that has endured to the present.

Tocino de cielo (rich caramel custard). This fine custard, popular in some places, consists of egg yolks mixed with heavy syrup and hardened in the oven. It is the ultimate dessert for anyone with a sweet tooth. Those who are not fond of sweets will certainly be quickly put off by this rich dessert.

Crema frita (fried custard squares). This pudding-like concoction, made with milk, flour, and egg yolks, should be of such a consistency that it will become solid when cooled. It is cut into slices, floured, and fried in pork lard.

Flan (custard). A very popular dessert, flan is seldom prepared properly. The mixture is made with milk, spiced with cinnamon and sugar, to which egg yolks are added. It is hardened in a water bath after being placed in a mold which has a layer of caramel at the bottom.

Throughout the Basque Country different fruit preserves are made,

as much in private homes as in commercial factories. Jams, jellies, syrups, and candied fruits are prepared in this way.

DAIRY PRODUCTS

Milk has been utilized since early times. The rural Basque has been a great consumer due to the fact that milk production is economical in the humid Cantabrian area. Fresh, boiled milk (*erreberri*) is very pleasant, but modern hygienic concerns have removed this from our diet.

We have already seen that milk often accompanies cereal porridges. Milk has been one of the principal nutritional staples of our people. It is the basis of various preparations which I will now cite.

Cuajada (mamia, curdled milk). Cuajada is an excellent food prepared with sheep's milk which is cooked and curdled at a temperature of about 37° C (98° F). The preparation of curdled milk in wooden vessels, originating from prehistoric times, produces an inevitable burned taste. Today, this taste can easily be avoided but is still in great demand.

Cuajada is one of the most nutritious and hygienic dishes. Not only is splendid nutrition provided by the sheep's milk, but it is served predigested due to the action of fermentation contained in the natural rennet.

Cottage cheese (gaztanbera). This food is similar to curds or farmer's cheese and is a by-product of cheese-making. It is obtained through cooking the whey that results from the coagulation of milk. It is then removed from the heat and the white substance floating on the top is removed. It is drained and molded.

Cheese (gazta). Cheese that is made from sheep's milk produced in our mountains is often excellent, so good that, even objectively, it may be said to reach the quality of the best cheeses of other countries.

Unfortunately it suffers from irregularity in quality. The cheese is

made in the most primitive and rudimentary of human shelters. Looking at a *txabola* (shepherd's hut) covered with sod (*zotalak*), it is easy to imagine prehistoric dwellings. In these huts, everything is done with less control than one would derive from even a limited experience. With the recent introduction of prepared rennet, a notable improvement in the product has occurred. Today, there are shepherds with a special instinct for cheese-making who produce good cheeses with more regularity than others.

In some areas, the cheeses are smoked. Good cheeses are as excellent fresh as aged and substitute quite well for the Italian cheeses used in the preparation of pasta dishes.

Quite excellent cheeses are usually found in Urbía, Aralar, Urbasa, and Roncal. There are no good cow's milk cheeses. In some industrial areas, however, foreign cheeses are imitated with good results.

Cheese is highly valued by the Basques, and the high prices it commands are a good indication of this esteem.

Butter (gurin). Butter is considered to be a luxury. The Fraisoro de la Diputación de Guipúzcoa and a few other industrial establishments do prepare good butter. Nonetheless, a good deal of inferior butter is eaten.

Much more butter is consumed in Labourd and the French continental areas of the Basque Country than on the Iberian Peninsula.

BEVERAGES

Wine is the most popular beverage and its growing diffusion is due to the improvements in transportation. *Chacolí* (*txakolin* in Basque), a light, acidic wine of excellent palate, is produced in the coastal areas.

In the Rioja region of Alava, wines of excellent quality are produced. With greater care taken in the cultivation of the vineyards and in the development of the vines, more consistent and uniform harvests are produced. These wines are distinct from the great French wines, but they can, in fact, compete with them.

Young wine (in the first year) from the Rioja is better than wine of the same age from Médoc or Burgundy. However, something prevents the Rioja, at fifteen years of age, from being of comparable palate to that of the French wine.

I think that it is time to stop saying that the French buy bad wines here in order to convert them into magnificent Chateau Margaux or Chateau Lagrange.

In Médoc, I have seen the care that is put into the cultivation of the vines and development of the wine, and I am certain that if we exercised as much technique and loving care, we would attain much of what they have attained.

What is said of the Rioja area can be applied to all the Basque wine-producing zones. The Rioja wines are of a fine palate and standard alcohol content. They are excellent table wines. The Navarrese wines have more body and alcohol content and less bouquet. When aged they accompany hearty dishes quite well.

The *chacolís*—wines of limited harvest obtained with difficulty due to the climate—are good wines to accompany fish. They bring to mind the wines of Moselle. The harvests from hot and dry summers are magnificent.

Those wines produced from the grape harvests of the Zarauz-Guetaria and Baquio regions have a well-deserved fame. In the French Basque Country excellent wines are also produced. The wines of Irouleguy, Belloc, and Saint-Étienne-de-Baigorry are famous.

For centuries cider was the most popular of our drinks. Consumption is declining every day, but it continues to be highly valued in various regions and served with some dishes, especially fish. Cider is also used as a flavoring in some recipes.

The best ciders are found in the lower part of Guipúzcoa. They are pale, dry ciders that do not irritate the stomach. Those of the upper region are sweeter and ironically called *andre-sagardo* (women's cider).

I cannot conclude this chapter without mentioning a concoction which is very popular in Vizcaya: lemonade combined with wine or *chacolí.* In the classic book *El Amparo,* we find this statement concerning the recipe for *limonada de vino blanco:* "La limonada, de limón . . . nada"—"lemonade" having almost nothing to do with lemons.

This concoction is diluted with watered wine and sugar and frozen. There are recipes in which various other ingredients are added.

Recipes

EDITOR'S NOTE

AS the reader will have determined, this volume is not a cookbook in the strictest sense. It is an orientation to traditional Basque cooking and its cultural context. The recipes that follow have been selected to highlight the unique characteristics of Basque food in the Old World.

Some of the ingredients listed in recipes may be difficult to obtain outside of the Basque Country. For instance, *chacolí,* a tart white wine of the region, is unique to the area; it spoils even if it travels to another part of Spain. Some varieties of fish used in the Basque recipes cannot be found in the U.S., although similar species can be obtained. Whenever possible, an appropriate substitution will be mentioned. And of course, individual cooks are encouraged to use their imagination.

Some ingredients are quite specific in Basque cooking. For instance, the variety of parsley used is always the flat Italian parsley, not the curly type more commonly found in markets in the U.S. The difference between the two is mainly in the strength of flavor. The Spanish Basques almost always use olive oil in their recipes instead of vegetable oil.

Many measurements of ingredients are listed in customary Ameri-

can form, followed by the original metric quantity. In some cases, we have provided only U.S. measurements when the original recipe did not list any specific amount. Several of the recipes do not include precise measurements of some ingredients. We believe that experienced cooks will be able to judge amounts for themselves in accordance with their own tastes.

For the reader's convenience, this English edition has included some instructions not found in the original Spanish volume—for example, a basic béchamel sauce to be used in the recipe for a cauliflower casserole. However, in other cases, such as the recipe for *natillas* (soft custard), the reader is not provided with extra information and is encouraged to use his or her own garnish (in this example, the meringue topping) with the basic dish.

Some traditional utensils used in Basque cooking are not available or are not practical for American cooks. For instance, the *cazuela,* an earthen casserole dish, is used frequently for frying and simmering on top of a wood stove. It does not work well on modern stoves or ranges. Cooks should use the utensils they would normally employ for the indicated cooking method.

The publisher would like to express its thanks to Jill Zubillaga, who devoted many hours to providing invaluable and much-needed assistance in making clear the instructions and ingredients of many of the recipes. She and her husband Joseph own the popular Santa Fe Hotel, a Basque restaurant in Reno, Nevada, and she is an excellent chef in her own right.

Contents

MEAT AND POULTRY

DESSERTS

VEGETABLES

Cabbage
Berza

For cabbage we do not offer rare or exotic recipes which would shock the palate. We can say, however, that a general defect in our preparation would be that of overcooking.

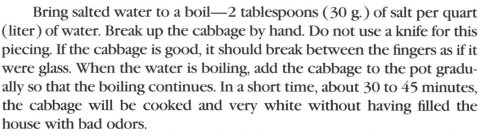

1 head loose-leaf cabbage	For flavoring:
water	pork ribs/Basque chorizo
salt	or
	garlic and olive oil

Bring salted water to a boil—2 tablespoons (30 g.) of salt per quart (liter) of water. Break up the cabbage by hand. Do not use a knife for this piecing. If the cabbage is good, it should break between the fingers as if it were glass. When the water is boiling, add the cabbage to the pot gradually so that the boiling continues. In a short time, about 30 to 45 minutes, the cabbage will be cooked and very white without having filled the house with bad odors.

There are two popular methods for seasoning cabbage. One is to cook pork ribs or Basque chorizo in the water before adding the cabbage. [You may leave the meat in with the cabbage if you so desire.] Another is to cook the cabbage, drain it, and add oil in which garlic has been browned. Perhaps this second method is the healthiest way of eating cabbage.

Cauliflower (*Coliflor*)

Cauliflower is cooked in a way similar to cabbage. However, we are not accustomed to eating it with pork.

Cauliflower Casserole
Budín de coliflor

This recipe is from the Marquesa de Parabere and is simply a pudding made of cooked cauliflower purée, béchamel sauce, and eggs.

1 head cauliflower
2 cups béchamel sauce
2 egg yolks
2 egg whites
butter

Béchamel sauce:
3 T. butter
3 T. flour
1 cup milk
½ cup light cream
1 tsp. salt
pinch of grated nutmeg
pinch of white or black
    pepper

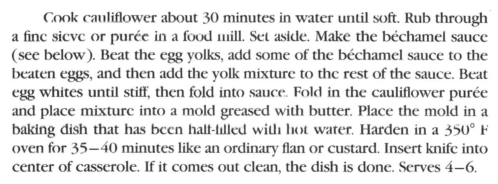

Cook cauliflower about 30 minutes in water until soft. Rub through a fine sieve or purée in a food mill. Set aside. Make the béchamel sauce (see below). Beat the egg yolks, add some of the béchamel sauce to the beaten eggs, and then add the yolk mixture to the rest of the sauce. Beat egg whites until stiff, then fold into sauce. Fold in the cauliflower purée and place mixture into a mold greased with butter. Place the mold in a baking dish that has been half-filled with hot water. Harden in a 350° F oven for 35–40 minutes like an ordinary flan or custard. Insert knife into center of casserole. If it comes out clean, the dish is done. Serves 4–6.

Béchamel sauce

Melt butter in a saucepan, add flour gradually, and cook for about a minute. Stir in milk, cream, salt, nutmeg, and pepper. Cook until thick.

Cardoon
Cardo

Cardoon is a member of the artichoke family, but its young stalks, when cooked, are similar in appearance to large celery. Good-quality cardoon is grown in the valley region of the Ebro River.

Cardoon is the most frequently consumed vegetable at Christmas dinners, and its preparation is unique.

1 cardoon bunch
water for boiling
lemon juice

Sauce:
1–2 tsp. olive oil per
**   serving**
several pieces of ham fat
**   or bacon**
½ clove garlic per
**   serving, sliced**
1–2 tsp. flour (equal
**   amount to oil)**

Begin with a cardoon which has become well whitened during cultivation and which fulfills the saying, *"El cardo y el queso al peso"* (Cardoon and cheese should be judged by weight).

Set a large pot of water to boil. Discard the tough outer stalks of the bunch. Add the remaining stalks to the boiling water. Do not cut them up any more than is required to fit them in the pot. Boil for 30 minutes, remove, and put in cold water.

Peel the cardoon and cut up into smaller sections, about 5 inches long. Set another pot of water to boil, and add a little lemon juice. Add the pieces of cardoon as the water is boiling and cook for 1½ hours. Today, this long cooking process can be avoided by placing the cardoon in a pressure cooker for 20 minutes. In either case, set aside some water used in the cooking for use in the sauce (see below). Pour sauce over the cardoon before serving.

Sauce

Put oil and ham fat in a frying pan and add garlic. Cook until the fat pieces float (through the action of the heat). Remove ham fat. Add a little flour and some of the water in which the cardoon has been cooked. Cook until a sauce is formed.

Broad Beans Vitoria Style
Habas verdes al estilo de Vitoria

This recipe is a simplified variation of the one presented by Elvira Arias de Apraiz in her book, *Libro de cocina,* the most widely known of all Basque cookbooks.

½ lb. (200 g.) very young broad beans, removed from their pods
2 oz. (50 g.) ham with fat on it (can substitute ham hocks or meaty slab bacon)
water for boiling

First, cook the ham for about an hour and a half in an amount of water that is just enough to cover the ham. While the water is boiling, add the beans little by little so that the water does not stop boiling.

The beans must always be covered with slowly boiling water; an excess of liquid should be avoided. They will be cooked in an hour if they are young and are not black at the tip.

Whatever broth is left is drained off and can be used in the preparation of vegetable purées. The beans are served together with the cut-up ham. One serving.

Tudelan Vegetable Pottage
Menestra de Tudela

The *menestra de Tudela* has achieved considerable fame due as much to the quality of garden produce that comprises it as to the fine skill applied in Tudela in its preparation.

There is no fixed formula for this preparation, which is essentially a vegetable pottage and a springtime dish. It is important that the ingredients be absolutely fresh and prepared soon after harvest.

Due to climatic conditions, some of the basic components—asparagus, baby artichokes, broad beans, green peas, and green beans—may be lacking. Other young vegetables may be included.

The vegetables should be stripped of their fibers so that the diner can easily digest the entire portion served.

Today, many preserved vegetables are used. Both canned and frozen, they may very well prove excellent but can never excite the taste buds as do the fresh products.

The process of making a typical *menestra* may seem peculiar to some readers, but each fresh vegetable should be cooked in a separate pot.

The various vegetables should be placed in boiling water gradually so as not to interrupt the boiling process.

Once cooked and tender, they are drained, with the exception of the asparagus. That water must be retained in case it is later necessary to add it to the sauce. The cooked vegetables are placed in a serving dish by layers and not stirred together.

The final touch is a sauce made in the following manner (amount per serving):

1½ T. (20 g.) olive oil
¼ medium (20 g.) onion, chopped
1 oz. (20–30 g.) chorizo, cut in thin rounds
½ oz. (10–15 g.) salt pork, diced
1 T. flour
1 cup dry white wine
some of the asparagus broth

In a frying pan on low heat add the oil, chopped onion, chorizo, and salt pork. When the onion begins to brown, add the flour and stir gently but thoroughly. When all is blended, add the cup of white wine and a little of the asparagus broth. Stir well while bringing the sauce to a boil. Then pour it over the cooked vegetables.

There is also something called the "deluxe" *menestra*—hard-boiled eggs and other garden produce are used as ingredients. But to our understanding, the authentic *menestra* of Tudela is made up of asparagus, baby artichokes, broad beans, and peas.

Potato and Leek Stew
Porrusalda

This leek and potato stew enjoyed great popularity until recently in extensive areas of the Basque Country. However, it is currently not as prevalent, now that new nutritional styles are being tried.

There are no fixed rules or recipes for its standardization, but two kinds of very different *porrusaldas* are worth presenting—one in which *bacalao* (codfish) is used and the other in which it is omitted. The recipe with *bacalao* provides a nutritionally complete dish—it includes animal proteins in addition to the abundant carbohydrates and the fat already contained in the basic dish.

Basic Porrusalda
(per serving)

½ lb. (220 g.) peeled potatoes	1½ T. (25 g.) olive oil
2 medium or 1 large leek(s)	1 whole clove garlic, minced
	boiling water

In a *cazuela* (an earthen casserole dish)—or substitute an iron skillet—brown the garlic in oil until golden. Cut up the leek and potato into good-sized pieces and add to pan. Fry for several minutes, then add boiling water until it covers the mixture. Cook until the potatoes and leeks are tender.

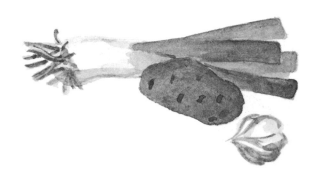

Porrusalda with Codfish

To the ingredients of the basic recipe, 2 oz. (50–60 g.) of dried, desalted codfish are added (per serving). The codfish is desalted by soaking it in water for twenty-four hours, and the remaining salty, lukewarm water is saved. Break cod into pieces.

This *porrusalda* is prepared according to the basic recipe, the difference being that the boiling water added to the mixture of fried potatoes and leeks *must be the water in which the cod has been soaked.* When this all comes to a boil, the fish pieces are added and left to boil for some time, together with the potatoes and leeks.

Potatoes in Wine
Patatas con vino

This is a genuine Alavese preparation which appears in the cook-book *Apuntes de cocina para uso de los hermanos carmelitas descalzos,* by Fr. G. de la Virgen del Carmen.

The good Carmelite monk must have been a great cook, following in the footsteps of Saint Theresa. She was also a Carmelite and, according to what can be read about her, a fine cook, in that "having a good hand at it, [she] placed much care in the task."

Since the book was printed in Vitoria, it seems obvious that the wine used by Fr. G. de la Virgen del Carmen was a standard one in Vitoria at that time, most likely a Rioja Alavesa. The recipe is excellent, according to my palate.

> **3 T. olive oil**
> **½ large onion**
> **½ lb. (200 g.) potatoes**
> **¼–½ cup Rioja Alavesa**
> **wine (red)**
> **salt to taste**

Brown onions in oil, taking care not to burn them. A light, golden-brown color is appropriate. Peel potatoes, cut up, and lightly fry in oil. Add red wine until potatoes are covered. Add salt and bring mixture to a boil. Serve when the potatoes are soft. One serving.

Garlic Soup Basque Style
Sopa con ajo a la vasca

1 large baguette dried French bread	4 eggs, beaten
4 T. (50 g.) pork lard	1 tsp. Spanish paprika (sweet or hot)
4 whole garlic cloves, peeled	water
	salt to taste

Heat lard in a skillet or earthen casserole dish. Lightly brown the whole, peeled garlic cloves; when golden add the sliced bread, paprika, salt, and water (enough to cover the bread). Leave this to simmer for 30 minutes. Before serving, add beaten eggs while stirring with a whisk. The egg will cook and form strands in the soup. Four servings.

EGGS

Basque Omelet
Piperrada Vasca

This is one of the best-known recipes outside of the Basque Country. Formerly, it was quite popular here, but perhaps due to the premium quality of peppers required for proper preparation, the dish is now not as common in some parts of the region.

Chefs of great renown such as Ignacio Domenech and Teodoro Bardají have sung the praises of this dish, in particular that which is prepared in Zarauz.

Biarritz and Saint-Jean-de-Luz are the Basque towns which have made this recipe popular with summer tourists. It is virtually unknown, however, in the peninsular Basque Country.

olive oil for frying
18 green Anaheim
    peppers (or 24 small
    peppers), cut into
    strips and with seeds
    removed
chopped onion and garlic
    for flavor
salt to taste

3 oz. salt pork, cut in
    small pieces
6 slices Bayonne or
    Pamplona ham (or
    smoked cooked ham)
3 large tomatoes
6 eggs, beaten
chopped Italian (flat)
    parsley

Place olive oil in a pan and add the green peppers, onion and garlic, and a little salt. Cook gradually so that the water given out by the peppers is evaporated.

In a separate pan, fry the pieces of salt pork and sliced ham. Remove the pork and ham, set aside, and slowly cook the tomatoes in the remaining grease. Add the tomatoes to the fried peppers.

Add the beaten eggs to the mixture, stir gently and slowly heat so that they do not curdle. (The eggs will set like a pudding.) Add the slices of fried ham and sprinkle with the chopped parsley. Serve from the pan by scooping out the portions with a spoon. Four servings.

NOTE: Individuals may want to increase the number of eggs used or reduce the number of peppers included in the recipe, according to their own taste.

Mushroom Omelet Alavese Style
Revuelto de perrechicos al estilo alavés

This is the most popular dish of Alavese cooking and is also appreciated in Vizcaya and Guipúzcoa. The preparation made in Alava, which is the best according to my taste, is as follows (amounts per serving):

¼ lb. (100 g.) mushrooms (*perrichicos* if possible)
1 egg, beaten
1 T. (10 g.) pork lard or bacon grease
salt to taste

Clean the mushrooms with a knife blade (or with a mushroom brush) without allowing them to be touched by water.

Perrechicos contain much fluid; it is necessary to remove this excess liquid in order not to ruin the omelet. To do this, piece them by hand without making the pieces too small. Place in a bowl, add salt, and set aside for 30 minutes.

Place mushrooms in a frying pan with the lard on low heat. Through the action of the heat, the natural juices of the mushrooms will be released and bathe the pieces.

Continue cooking slowly until the water has evaporated, then add the beaten egg and stir continuously until the mixture begins to harden. Remove from heat.

It should be noted that this is an omelet in the French style and not a *tortilla española* (a potato omelet). It should be similar to *oeufs brouillés* (scrambled eggs). It must remain very soft—*baboso* or "runny," as they say in Alava. This is an excellent dish as much for its aroma as for its appearance and taste.

In Guipúzcoa they cut up mushrooms in fine slices that are fried and then added to the egg. This method is not to be criticized, but it does not equal the quality of the Alavese recipe.

FISH AND SEAFOOD

Fish Stew
Tioro

    As mentioned in the main text, this fine Labourdin dish is more complicated than most Basque recipes for fish soups and stews. It includes frying, boiling, sieving, and again boiling. The ingredients listed are for four servings:

8 pieces of fish—
    merluza (hake),
    pezcarilla (small
    hake), or *rape* (angler)
olive oil for frying
2 onions (can also use
    leeks)
a handful of herbs (bay
    leaf, tarragon, Italian
    parsley, etc.)
2 T. tomato purée

1 cup *chacolí* or dry
    white wine
sugar to taste
fish stock
cayenne and black
    pepper
curry (optional)
shrimp, lobster, squid, or
    shellfish such as
    mussels
8 slices French bread

In a large skillet, slowly fry the fish in oil. Remove from pan and set aside. Add the onions, leeks, and herbs to the oil and fry. Add the tomato purée and stir. Soak the mixture with *chacolí* and simmer for a while. If the sauce has a bitter taste, add a little sugar. Add some fish stock and then pass the mixture through a fine sieve or food processor.

Place the pieces of fish in a dutch oven and add the sauce. Cook the stew at a slow boil. Spices such as cayenne and black pepper should be added. A small amount of curry may also go well with this dish. Squid, shrimp, lobster, or shellfish should be added to the pot and cooked about 15 minutes before serving. Brown the slices of French bread in oil and add to the stew as it is served.

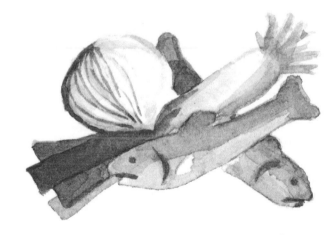

Tuna of the Pelota Player
Atún o bonito a la pelotari

    This popular tuna recipe has many names and has been presented in various tuna competitions under different designations.

    Ana María Calera, in her extremely complete work *La cocina vasca,* provides us with a standardized recipe which we present with slight variations that do not alter its magnificence.

2 lbs. (1 kilo) fresh tuna
    or bonito, boned and
    skinned
2 T. (30 ml.) olive oil
3 onions (100 g.), sliced
3 whole garlic cloves,
    minced
bay leaf to taste (only a
    little is needed)
fresh oregano to taste
black pepper to taste
chopped Italian parsley
    to taste
2 whole cloves, crushed
1 whole shallot or
    scallion

Sauce:
4 oz. (100 g.) lard or
    hardened bacon grease
½ regular or 1 small
    onion, chopped
1 sprig Italian parsley,
    chopped
2 T. flour
1 cup *chacolí* or dry
    white wine
salt to taste
pepper to taste
1 slice lemon
4 raw egg yolks, beaten
1 dozen good-sized
    mushrooms, chopped
1 shallot

Place the tuna in a marinade of the oil, onion, garlic, bay leaf, oregano, black pepper, parsley, cloves, and shallot. Soak 3–4 hours, turning from time to time.

While the tuna is marinating, the sauce may be prepared. Melt the lard in a large skillet and fry the chopped onion. When it begins to color, add the chopped parsley. When the onion is browned (without burning), add the flour. Then add the *chacolí,* salt, pepper, and lemon slice. Let the mixture simmer for 30 minutes.

Remove sauce from heat and cool to lukewarm. Add some of the warm liquid to the beaten egg yolks, then add the yolk mixture, the shallot, and the mushrooms to the rest of the sauce. Stir well and bring mixture to a slow boil again. Leave on low heat to reduce the sauce.

Remove the tuna from the marinade, drain on cloth or paper towels. The chunks of tuna should be roasted until done—on a grill set over coals, if possible. (Grease the grill to prevent sticking or wrap fish in aluminum foil. If roasting is not possible, fry the tuna in butter.) Serve the tuna with the completed sauce. Six servings.

The ideal accompaniment for this dish is a good, dry *chacolí,* the best ones being from Guctaria or Baquio.

NOTE: Oregano is not common in Basque cooking. If desired, substitute thyme.

Tuna Stew
Marmitako de Currito

My dear friend Currito of Santurce, winner of numerous *marmitako* contests, supplies us with his recipe, which I dare to present to my readers, even without his permission. However, I know that because he is generous, he would agree to whatever benefits the public.

In further justification of my attitude, I would add that although I provide Currito's authentic recipe, I realize that it would prove difficult to achieve the level of excellence usually reached by the master. I myself can attest to this, having been a member of the judging team in contests in which Currito has participated.

3 whole onions	**Vizcayan sauce:**
3⅓ lbs. (1½ kilos) tuna or bonito	**12 *choricero* peppers (dry, red peppers)**
3⅓ lbs. (1½ kilos) potatoes, peeled	**water**
6 whole green Anaheim peppers	**2 lbs. (1 kilo) tomatoes, peeled and chopped**
1 whole leek	**1 lb. (½ kilo) onions, chopped**
½ cup (100 g.) olive oil	**olive oil for frying**
water	**6 cloves garlic, chopped**
3 scoops (ladles) Vizcayan sauce	**2 oz. (50 g.) bread**
salt to taste	**1 T. paprika**

Take two of the onions, chop well, place in a *marmita* (large pot) with the olive oil, and fry on a high flame until golden. Meanwhile, in a

separate pot full of water, place the tail and head of the fish, the leek (cut in half), two of the green Anaheim peppers (sliced lengthwise), and the other whole onion, peeled. Bring the broth to a boil and let simmer.

Finely chop the remaining four Anaheim peppers, cut the potatoes into pieces, and add to the pot of frying onions. Stir well for a few minutes. Add enough of the fish broth from the other pot to cover the potatoes. When the potatoes are well cooked, add the Vizcayan sauce (preparation follows).

Cut the tuna into pieces and add to the above mixture. Add salt to taste. Stir well and boil for 2–4 minutes. This stew may be left to sit up to two hours; after that time, the potatoes will harden. Before serving, heat again. Six servings.

(Most other recipes for *marmitako* add the fish when the potatoes are added to cook in the broth. Water is used instead of fish stock.)

Vizcayan sauce

Soak the *choriceros* 1½ hours in enough hot water to cover the peppers. Then cut the peppers in half, remove the stems and seeds, and retain the pulp. Chop well.

Fry the onions and garlic in olive oil. Add small pieces of bread, the paprika, and the peppers. Stir well. Add tomatoes, then the water used to soak the peppers. Cook for 35 minutes. Pass mixture through a food mill.

NOTE: This recipe for *salsa vizcaina* has been added to the English edition. The reader should also refer to the author's description of Vizcayan sauce included in the discussion of cod in the main text. Busca Isusi, among others, felt that the true *salsa vizcaina* does not include tomatoes.

Sea Bass San Sebastián Style
Mero a la donostiarra

6 steaks (center cut) sea
    bass—about 4 lbs.
    (2 kilos)
butter remaining from
    sauce preparation
flour
salt
2 jiggers Scotch whiskey

Garnish (suggested):
grilled cherry tomatoes
mashed potatoes
small triangles of bread

Sauce:
4 large onions
2 large carrots
2 cups (½ liter) olive oil
1 lb. (400 g.) angler (a
    whitefish) center cut
1 tail of small lobster
¾ lb. (300 g.) shrimp
1 lb. (400 g.) fresh
    mushrooms
3 jiggers cognac
2 lbs. (1 kilo) canned
    tomatoes
2 T. (25 g.) concentrated
    beef bouillon
sugar to taste
salt to taste
14 oz. (400 g.) cream
½ lb. (200 g.) butter
1 clove garlic, minced

Sauce

Finely chop onions and carrots and place in a skillet with the olive oil, over low heat. When the mixture is half-cooked, add half the quantities of angler, lobster tail, shrimp, and mushrooms, all cut into small pieces. Cook for twenty minutes.

Add the cognac and flame the mixture. Then break up and add the tomatoes, along with the bouillon and a little sugar to eliminate acidity. Salt to taste. Cook for 30 minutes over low heat.

Add the cream and continue cooking for about 10 minutes in order to reduce the sauce. Pass the remaining sauce through a food mill or blender and place in a double boiler over low heat.

Sauté the remaining shrimp, angler, mushrooms, and lobster tail (all cut into pieces) in a wide saucepan with some of the butter and the minced garlic. Remove the seafood and mushroom pieces from the pan and add to the sauce.

Fish

Twenty minutes before serving, add the remaining butter to the saucepan. Lightly flour and salt the fish steaks and place in the butter. Turn after ten minutes of cooking. Add whiskey. After ten more minutes, remove from heat, drain off the emitted juices, pour through a strainer, and add this juice to the already prepared sauce.

To serve, place the fish steaks in an oval serving dish and cover with the sauce. The plate may be garnished with grilled cherry tomatoes, some mashed potatoes, and small triangles of bread. Six servings.

(With this plate, Jesús Rodero of the Hotel Maisonave in Pamplona won first place in the professional chefs' contest.)

Sea-Bream Bermeo Style
Besugo al estilo de Bermeo

This recipe by Ignacio Domenech is called *Bixigua Bermeo'ko eraz* in Basque. (In the U.S., red snapper may be substituted for the red sea-bream.)

1 sea-bream, 2–3 lbs. (1,000–1,300 g.)
salt
pepper
olive oil
7–8 garlic cloves
2 T. wine vinegar

Clean and scale the sea-bream, season with a little salt and pepper, and soak in a good olive oil for a while. Make small cuts reaching through to the main backbone.

Twenty minutes before serving, roast the fish on a grill over a low flame, basting it with oil. (Grease the grill to prevent sticking, or use a grill basket for fish.)

If the sea-bream is on the large side, prepare a sauce to be served with it. Place a small cup of olive oil in a frying pan on the stove. Fry seven or eight garlic cloves and remove from heat when these are golden. Crush in a mortar or garlic press and mix gradually with the warm oil. Add two tablespoons of wine vinegar and a little salt, and stir well.

Place the sea-bream, just roasted on the grill, on a hot serving platter and pour the garlic and oil sauce over it. Five to six servings.

Scad (Horse Mackerel) with Tomato Sauce
Chicharros con tomate

4 mackerel	olive oil for frying
salt	2 lbs. (1 kilo) fresh or
1 lb. (½ kilo) onion,	canned tomatoes
chopped	Italian (flat) parsley,
5 cloves garlic, minced	finely chopped

Clean the fish thoroughly, season them with salt, and place in refrigerator for two hours.

Add olive oil to a skillet and fry the onion and garlic until golden. Then add the tomatoes and cook thoroughly. Purée in a food mill or processor.

Pour the purée into a large skillet and place the mackerel on top of it. Dust with the finely chopped parsley. Cover and cook slowly until the fish are tender. Place the mackerel in a serving dish and pour the tomato purée over them. Four servings.

Hake in Green Sauce
Merluza en salsa verde

2 lbs. (1 kilo) hake
1¼ cups (300 ml.) olive oil
3–6 garlic cloves, minced (amount according to taste)
fresh Italian parsley, finely chopped
salt to taste

Clean the hake and cut into steaks (rounds) about ¾ inch (2 cm.) thick. Season with salt.

Add the olive oil to a large skillet and fry the minced garlic over low heat. It is traditional to use a *cazuela* (clay casserole dish) large enough so that all the fish steaks fit into it with a little room left over. When the garlic, through the action of the heat, begins to turn golden and float, remove the pan from the heat. Quickly place the fish in it, sprinkle with finely chopped parsley, and return the pan to low heat.

Soon you will notice white spots of a milky substance appearing on the pieces of hake. Begin to move the casserole in a constant, circular motion, or better yet, back and forth.

After some time, you will see that the fluid emitted from the fish joins with the oil to form a thick sauce. This is the genuine *salsa verde* (green sauce). Continue moving the pan for a little while. While the fish is still cooking, sample the sauce and add salt to taste. When all the fish slices reach the same white color, the dish is ready for the table. Six servings.

This sauce has many names within Basque cooking—most were introduced by chefs for their own variations—but basically, *salsa verde* is as described above. (This preparation method is sometimes confused with the *al pil-pil* procedure.)

Within the last fifty years, *kokotxas en salsa verde* has acquired fame. (*Kokotxas—kokotxak* in Basque—are the long, translucent, gelatinous parts of the hake cut from the throat region. It is still the most valued and delicate part of this fish.) Rockfish such as *sargo* or sheephead fish are also quite good in *salsa verde*.

According to Basque taste, the drink which best accompanies such dishes is cider served at wine-cellar temperature (50°–55° F, 10°–13° C). The white *chacolí* is also favored, in that it is an acidic and dry wine served at about 43° F (8° C).

Codfish Club Ranero
Bacalao al Club Ranero

This is a great codfish recipe, eaten in the spring, and it is continually gaining converts. It is not a new dish; in cooking it is practically impossible to invent or discover anything new. This dish is simply the combination of codfish, together with a fried mixture, which occurred to a French chef named Alejandro Caveriviere, who at one time participated in the Sociedad Bilbaína (a gastronomic society) and wanted to leave something behind to commemorate his departure.

1½ lbs. (600 g.) dried salted codfish, cut into strips

4 medium (600 g.) tomatoes, peeled, seeded, and chopped

4 medium Spanish yellow onions, chopped

3 garlic cloves, finely chopped

3 *cristal* peppers (roasted red peppers), cut in large squares

6 *nora* or *choricero* peppers (dry, red peppers), pulp only

1 sprig Italian parsley, chopped

½ cup (125 ml.) olive oil

Desalt the codfish by soaking for 24 hours in water, changing the water 3–4 times. Drain and press firmly to remove all of the water. Prepare the *nora* or *choricero* peppers by soaking 1½ hours in enough hot water to cover the peppers, then cutting in half and removing the stems and seeds. Retain the pulp and chop well.

Combine the tomatoes, onions, garlic, *cristal* peppers, and parsley and fry slowly in olive oil. The pieces of tomato should remain intact at low heat. When the onion is tender, add the pulp of the *choricero* peppers. Drain off and set aside the liquid from the mixture. Remove pan from heat.

Lay the codfish strips on top of the fried mixture. Beat liquid that was set aside until it is creamy and the oil is completely blended. Pour the sauce over the codfish and place over low heat. Gently move the pan around so that the sauce covers the fish. Cook slowly until the fish is done—about 15–30 minutes.

This delicacy is now ready for the table. Six servings.

NOTE: Roast the fresh red peppers by placing under preheated broiler about 3 inches from heat until browned and blistered. Turn and roast other side until peppers are completely charred. Place in a bowl and cover; allow to steam for 5 minutes. Place under running water and peel.

Peppers Stuffed with Cod
Pimientos rellenos de bacalao

The recipe for this dish was presented by doña Carmen O. de Ruiz de Garibay, who received second prize in the "Contest for Housewives" of Alimentación '75.

6 fresh whole red peppers, roasted and peeled
1 lb. (½ kilo) dried codfish
1 whole potato, peeled
1 whole green Anaheim pepper
2 cloves garlic, chopped
1 cup (200 g.) olive oil

8 oz. (1 small can) tomato sauce
1 small onion, finely chopped
½ tsp. flour
1 cup water
black pepper to taste (optional)
cayenne pepper to taste (optional)

Piece the codfish and soak in water 24 hours to remove salt (change the water 3–4 times). Drain fish by pressing the pieces down firmly to remove all of the water.

Remove the stems from the fresh red peppers and make a small hole at that end. Remove the seeds and singe the peppers on a metal grill (or under a broiler). This action aids in peeling them (see footnote for Codfish Ranero). Peel and set aside.

Cut the potato and green pepper into very small pieces and fry them slowly. In a separate pan, fry the chopped garlic in enough of the olive oil for cooking the fish. When the garlic begins to brown and the oil is hot enough, add the codfish and fry slowly, stirring it for a while. Add the fried potato and green pepper, along with 2 or 3 tablespoons of tomato sauce. Cook for one minute on low heat, stirring continuously to avoid any sticking. Stuff the codfish mixture into the red peppers that have been set aside and place them in a large skillet.

Make a sauce by lightly frying the finely chopped onion in olive oil. When the onion is golden, add flour and stir so that it also becomes golden. Add a cup of water and a little more tomato sauce. Black and/or cayenne pepper may also be added to the sauce. Pour over stuffed peppers.

Cook the stuffed peppers slowly in the sauce until done, turning them frequently. If the sauce thickens too much, add a little water or broth. Six servings.

NOTE: For an additional recipe using codfish, see the entry for potato and leek stew—*porrusalda.*

Turbot in Green Sauce
Rodaballo en salsa verde

½ lb. (250 g.) turbot, per serving
3 T. (50 cc.) olive oil
½ clove garlic, minced

flat (Italian) parsley, finely chopped
hot red pepper (or paprika) to taste

This recipe is very similar to that of the hake, with the difference being in the cut of the fish. Once cleaned and carefully scraped, the turbot is filleted.

Place the olive oil and garlic in a skillet over low heat. When the garlic begins to turn golden as a result of the heat, it should float; at this time, take the pan off the heat. Place the pieces of fish in the skillet along with the chopped parsley and put back over the heat. In a short while, white spots of plasma (a milky substance) appear on the fish. Begin to move the pan back and forth in a continuous motion. After some time, you will notice that the fluid emitted from the pieces of fish has joined with the oil to form a thick sauce; this is the authentic *salsa verde*.

Continue the back-and-forth movement for a short while. When the fish slices are white, the dish is ready to be served. Red pepper or paprika may be sprinkled over the preparation. One serving.

There are those who adorn this dish with cooked garden vegetables in season: peas, broad beans, asparagus, and artichokes. In this case, a little water is added to the sauce while cooking so that it all holds together well.

Salmon from the Bidasoa Region
Salmón del Bidasoa de Casa de la Patxa en Lesaka

The main secret of this salmon recipe (by Manuel Sarobe y Pueyo) from the Bidasoa region is in the cleaning of the fish. The most important thing is a total cleaning, eliminating guts and blood without injuring the meat. To accomplish this, all intestines and blood must be extracted from the anal orifice. It must be noted that salmon, if cooked in slices, loses the gelatin which gives it flavor, juiciness, and aroma. Because of this, its cleaning is a very difficult, slow, and delicate process, taking into account that the salmon has a large quantity of blood. The home method consists of utilizing as an extractor the hook which is at the end of ladles and kitchen utensils. Once cleaned, a linen or cotton cloth is prepared, and on top of it is placed a bed of vegetables including carrots, onions, leeks, parsley, and four or five cloves of garlic, together with lemon, all cut into slices or rounds. The salmon is placed on top of the vegetables and then covered with more vegetables. Everything is wrapped up well in the cloth, tied with a cord, and put into a special receptacle called a *salmonera* (a fish poacher) and containing some cold water, salt, unrefined oil, and a glass of white wine. There are some who also add two or three tablespoons of vinegar and spices. In the oven, it is necessary to watch it carefully, and when the water is heated it is kept in the first stage of cooking—that is to say, it continues cooking without the water actually coming to a boil. The cooking time for a salmon of 11 pounds (5 kilos) is approximately 30 minutes. Once cooked, it must be left out to cool down in the same water until it is completely cold. It is then served on a wooden tray covered with ferns and accompanied by mayonnaise, tartar sauce, and vinaigrette.

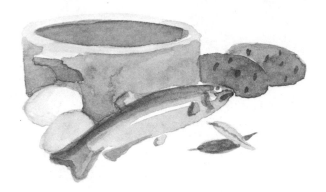

Trout a la Navarra
Truchas a la Navarra

4 trout, 9–12 oz.
  (250–350 g.) each
2 eggs, beaten
olive oil
10 oz. red wine
salt
black pepper

1 onion, finely chopped
1 sprig mint
thyme
rosemary
1 laurel (bay) leaf

Place the cleaned trout in a clay casserole. Mix together the chopped onion, red wine, a little black pepper, a sprig of mint, thyme, rosemary, and the bay leaf. Pour the mixture over the trout and let marinate for one hour.

Put the casserole over medium-low heat (or transfer the trout and marinade to a skillet), adding a splash of olive oil and salt to taste. When the broth has been reduced, remove the trout and pass the broth through a strainer. Add some of the warm liquid to the beaten eggs, blend, and then add the eggs to the rest of the broth. Beat together and pour over the trout. Four servings.

This preparation (a recipe of Manuel Sarobe y Pueyo) is served with boiled potatoes.

Peppers Stuffed with Spider Crab
Pimientos del piquillo de Lodosa rellenos de txangurro

This is a delicious recipe in Basque cuisine which combines small green peppers (*pimientos del piquillo*) from the Navarrese town of Lodosa with a crab stuffing typically prepared for *txangurro a la donostiarra.*

According to my information, it was the concept of the chefs Arzak and Roteta. I myself can attest to the great success that this recipe had in a dinner prepared in the Hotel Melia Castilla. It was served by Juan Mari Arzak on the occasion of the First European Convention of Gastronomic Journalists, Writers, and Editors, held in Madrid on October 24–27, 1981.

3 whole *pimientos del piquillo* from Lodosa (or substitute small Anaheim peppers) per serving, fresh or canned

stuffing used in *txangurro a la donostiarra*
3½ T. (50 cc.) cream

Clean and roast the small peppers (see recipe of codfish Club Ranero for roasting method). Prepare the stuffing. Use a soup spoon to fill two peppers per serving with the stuffing.

To one side, finely chop the third pepper by hand or grind by machine. add cream and heat slowly. Run this mixture through a food mill or blender. Pour the resulting sauce over the stuffed peppers and heat (350° F for about 15 minutes).

Spider Crab San Sebastián Style
Txangurro a la donostiarra

1 spider crab, medium-
sized (3 lbs., 1½ kilos),
live
3 leeks, white section
only
1 medium onion (100 g.),
peeled
2 large carrots (200 g.),
peeled
fresh ground white
pepper, to taste
(cayenne pepper has
been used in the past)
olive oil

butter
4 T. (60 g.) tomato paste,
fresh or canned
1 jigger cognac (not
brandy)
1 cup sherry
spices to taste
4 oz. (1 small coffee cup)
clear broth (fish stock)
5 T. (75 g.) cream
1 T. bread crumbs
Italian parsley, well
chopped
2 cloves garlic, minced

Add two of the leeks, one carrot, and a piece of the onion to a pot of water, along with the cayenne or white pepper. When the water is at full boil, submerge the live crab, cover, and return to a boil. There should be enough water to cover the crab completely during its cooking. Boil for 20 minutes, then remove from the heat and leave to cool.

When the crab is cooled, remove the meat from the legs and body. This is necessary so that the meat is not greatly reduced through shrinkage. Save the shell. Cut crab into small pieces.

Fry the remaining leek, the other carrot, and the rest of the onion in oil and butter, taking care that they do not burn. When the onion is tender, add the diced pieces of crab and stir well. Mix in the tomato paste, cognac, sherry, spices, some clear broth, and the cream. This mixture should end up as a thick and savory mass. Take care not to add too much broth.

Fill the shell of the crab with the thick mixture. Add the chopped parsley and garlic to the bread crumbs and sprinkle over the crab. Dot with butter and bake in a hot oven (400° F) until crusty (about 10 minutes).

This is a magnificent dish along the lines of *langouste à l'Américaine*. We Basques already had it in our repertory when chef Pierre Fraisse introduced the famous French dish.

Squid in Its Own Ink
Chipirones en su tinta

These squid are also called *txipiroiak* and *jibiones* in various parts of the Basque Country. In the rest of Spain, they are referred to as *calamares*.

2 lbs. (1 kilo) small fresh
    whole squid with ink
    sacs (caught with
    hooks)
1 onion, finely chopped
1 clove garlic, finely
    chopped
olive oil for frying
Italian (flat) parsley,
    chopped
bread crumbs

Sauce:
1 onion, finely chopped
1 clove garlic, finely
    chopped
crust of bread
1–2 T. fish broth
ink from the sacs
8 T. tomato purée

Take apart and clean the fresh squid, taking great care to remove the ink sacs without breaking them. (For a detailed description of the cleaning method, see other cookbooks, for example Peter Feibleman, *The Cooking of Spain and Portugal,* Time-Life Books, 1969, p. 121.) Set the ink sacs aside. Cut the tentacles into one-inch chunks.

Fry one onion and one garlic clove, both finely chopped, in olive oil. When the onion begins to take on color, add the chunks of squid tentacles and cook slowly while stirring in the oil. Add the chopped parsley and bread crumbs and stir until well thickened.

Stuff the squid tails with this mixture, being careful not to overfill. Seal the openings with a toothpick. Fry the stuffed tails in a small amount of olive oil, turning gently, until golden in color. Meanwhile make the ink sauce (see below).

Place the sauce in a large skillet, add the fried, stuffed squid and simmer for 15 minutes. Three to four servings.

This dish is usually served with slices of French bread that have been fried in olive oil. It is very aromatic and flavorful. The recipe diminishes in quality if netted or frozen squid are used. Always question the authenticity of a squid dish when it is offered out of season.

Ink sauce

Brown the one onion and the garlic clove in olive oil, and add a crust of bread. Place the fish broth in a small bowl or cup. Place the reserved ink sacs in a fine sieve over the bowl and puncture carefully. Blend the ink and broth. Add this liquid to the onion and garlic and cook slowly. Add the tomato purée and continue to simmer for a short time. Run the mixture through a food processor or blender.

MEAT AND POULTRY

Blood Sausages
Buzkantzak

As there are now few houses which slaughter a whole lamb (*bil-dots*), I have changed to familiar and common measurements the old recipes that depended on approximations according to the size of the animal.

In the first place it must be assured that the animal is young and grain-fed. The two-year-old castrated male, considerably fattened, is ideal. Besides having fat and blood of first quality, it also provides us with high-quality meat for other preparations. The young sterile lambs are also excellent. Here is an excellent old recipe.

13 lbs. (6 kilos) onions, not sweet

18 large leeks, white part only

4½ lbs. (2 kilos) fat from the kidney and peritoneum, or lard

2½ quarts (2½ kilos) uncoagulated blood

6 hot red peppers, very finely chopped

1 oz. (*papeleta*) dried, ground clove

1 oz. (*papeleta*) dried, ground anise

3 oz. (*papeletas*) ground black pepper

3 oz. (*papeletas*) dried, ground oregano

1 oz. (*papeleta*) ground cinnamon

salt to taste

Chop the onions and leeks very finely and cook slowly for about ten hours in lard or a little fat from the animal. As the mixture is heating, the onions and leeks will release the natural vegetable juices in which they will continue cooking. If the temperature is raised significantly, the abundant sugars in the onion can caramelize and even burn, something which should be avoided at all costs. After this cooking, the mixture should be like a thick purée of a creamy, brown color.

Chop the remaining fat very finely and place in a separate container. Mix in the blood, completely integrating the two ingredients. Then mix in the purée of onions and leeks. It is advantageous to combine these mixtures in a clay receptacle surrounded by lukewarm water. Otherwise, the fat remains hardened and mixes badly.

Add the chopped peppers and spices and mix again to distribute uniformly. Stuff this mixture into cleaned intestines and stomach (or sausage casings) and scald until the mixture is well coagulated.

Prepare a broth with leeks and a little fresh fat and cook the sausages for 30 minutes at a slow boil. (With the broth left from the cooking of the sausages, it is the custom to prepare soup accompanied by slices of bread.)

Buzkantzak (also called *odolkiak*) can be simply boiled before being eaten. They can be baked or fried and are also excellent when cooked in cabbage or with beans.

Because these sausages are very fatty and strong tasting, they should not be eaten accompanied by water or weak wines. In the Rioja region—as much in Alava as in Castilla and Navarra—there are red wines that go wonderfully well with these blood sausages.

NOTE: *Papeleta* refers to the usual minimum quantity of each spice that is sold commercially in the Basque Country. Wrapped in a small paper, it is equivalent to about one ounce (30 grams).

Lamb in Chilindrón Sauce
Cordero al chilindrón

Chilindrón is a preparation which normally is used for all types of tender meats, such as lamb, rabbit, chicken, and young pork. It is a dish which pertains to towns located on both sides of the Ebro River, in Basque and non-Basque zones alike.

The word *chilindrón* is not accepted by the Spanish Language Academy other than as a term used to denote a game of cards or as a *chirca,* a type of South American tree. Related to the word *chilindrón* is *chilindrina,* meaning a trifle or thing of insignificance.

The culinary expert who deals most with the *chilindrón* is Teodoro Bardají, who says that this preparation finds a precedent in Aragonese and Navarrese cooking—I would add Alavese cooking as well.

The following recipe is from the great Alavese chef, Elvira Arias de Apraiz.

1 front quarter lamb
   (3 lbs. or 1,300 g.)
1 whole onion
lard
1 T. flour
1 cup cognac
2 young garlic cloves,
   chopped

ground red pepper
   (cayenne)
1 roasted pepper
   (*pimiento
   calahorrano*)
vinegar

Cut the quarter of lamb into pieces. Chop the onion and add to the lard (fry slowly until the onion is golden). Add the pieces of lamb and then the flour.

In another dish, combine the cognac, cayenne pepper, garlic, roasted pepper, and a little vinegar. Pass the mixture through a food mill (blender) and pour over the lamb. Place the dish over low heat and simmer until the lamb is tender.

NOTE: The cognac referred to is undoubtedly a brandy from Jerez. The lamb is surely from the region of Treviño. Lamb raised in that region is the best, according to my palate. (The reader will note that most other *chilindrón* recipes include tomatoes or tomato sauce.)

Tolosan Veal Tongue
Lengua de ternera a la tolosana

This is a magnificent recipe of Guipuzcoan cuisine which Teodoro Bardají provides in his fine work *La cocina de ellas.* It is a very popular dish in Tolosa, especially on those Mondays when the town fair is held. The great chef says: "A dish of tongue, somewhat complicated in its preparation, but well worth the effort due to the truly extraordinary portions and results. I am unsure if it is native to Guipúzcoa; I can only be assured of the fact that in Tolosa, the ancient capital of the province, it is prepared in most restaurants on market days [Saturdays]. A large number of *casheros* [rural people] are in town at that time to complete their transactions."

2 veal tongues
salt
pepper
onions, carrots, leeks,
   and garlic cloves, all
   sliced in rounds
2 cloves, mashed (or
   equivalent in ground
   cloves)

1 bay leaf, crushed
olive oil or pork fat
1 cup white wine
4–5 tomatoes, cut in
   pieces
water
flour
egg, beaten

Wash the tongues thoroughly in cold water, scrubbing them with a coarse vegetable brush. In a large pot or dutch oven, prepare a bed of sliced onions, carrots, leeks, and garlic. Salt and pepper the tongues and place them on top of the vegetables. Add the mashed cloves and bay leaf and sprinkle with hot oil or melted pork fat. Cover the pot and cook over low heat until the vegetables begin to brown. Turn the tongues to brown evenly on all sides.

Drain off the fat or oil and then add the white wine. As the wine evaporates over the heat, add the tomato pieces and enough water to cover the tongues.

Cook only until the tongues are tender. If overcooked, they will be somewhat tough. Remove from the heat when almost done and allow to cool down before peeling. The tongues will be easier to peel if they are still warm. Cut the tongues in thin slices and dip into flour and then beaten egg. Fry the slices in very hot oil or lard until quite brown.

Place the slices in a wide pan or skillet. Pass the broth in which the tongue was cooked through a strainer. Better yet, pass it through a food mill so that the vegetable purée will thicken the broth. Pour over the sliced tongue and simmer slowly for 15 minutes. Taste and correct for seasoning. Eight servings.

Roasted peppers are a good accompaniment to this dish.

The sauce of this dish should be thick but still fluid. The tongues can be scalded and then peeled before cooking, but in that case, they will be more cooked near the surface, making it more difficult to cut them into slices. Peeling the tongues after they have been cooked makes them easier to cut, and they are tender on all sides.

Hash
Hachua de Espelette

This is a typical dish of the French town of Espelette in the north of the Basque Country. It is famous for its peppers and its *hachua*.

The basis of this dish is ox, beef, or veal. The meat is very lean (all fat is removed). The ham usually used is the Bayonne ham, but the Serrano or Jabugo ham would also serve the purpose quite well.

½ lb. (200 g.) ham with salt-cured bacon
2 onions, chopped
2 garlic cloves, minced
some flour
4 small sprigs aromatic herbs

2½ cups (600 cc.) bouillon
1⅓ lbs. (600 g.) lean meat, cut into medium-sized pieces
green peppers

In a stew pot or dutch oven, separate bacon from ham; place the bacon on low heat and cook down. Add the chopped onion and minced garlic. Next, cut the ham into pieces and brown in the fat. Add the flour and herbs and stir well. Before the flour browns, add the bouillon. Cook until the sauce thickens and let bubble a little, then add the pieces of meat. Cover, place on low heat, and cook gradually for 2½ hours until the meat is tender. Four servings.

While the meat is cooking, there will be time to fry or roast the peppers. If the peppers are large, they should be roasted and peeled. After frying or roasting, cut them into strips and add to the main pot.

Pork Loin in Milk
Lomo de cerdo con leche

This original method for preparing pork loin was well accepted in former times, but today it is used infrequently—without a doubt due to the length of time required for the meat to be properly done. The more rapid methods of frying or roasting the pork loin are more popular today, and grilling is especially preferred.

This recipe is ideally prepared in an earthenware pot.

2 lbs. (800 g.) pork loin	**milk**
4 oz. (100 g.) pork lard	**white pepper to taste**
2 garlic cloves, minced	

Melt the lard in a skillet and brown the pork loin. Transfer the pork to the pot in which it will cook and add the garlic. Add enough milk to cover the meat and sprinkle lightly with white pepper.

Cook slowly over low heat for about an hour until the milk takes on a yellow tone and begins to thicken. Remove the meat, let cool, and cut into thin slices. Place on a serving platter and cover with the sauce from the pot. Four servings. (The author allows ½ pound of meat per serving.)

Peppers Stuffed with Meat
Pimientos rellenos de carne

This recipe, presented by doña Usua Busca, was awarded a first prize in the Housewives' Contest of Alimentación '75.

Stuffing:
several large red peppers
  (*pimientos del pico*),
  roasted and peeled
  (one per serving)
2 medium onions
  (200 g.), finely chopped
2 garlic cloves, minced
pork lard for frying
1 lb. (400 g.) ground pork
  meat
salt
pepper
4 oz. (1 sm. coffee cup)
  white wine
1 whole egg
2 egg yolks

1 T. bread crumbs soaked
  in milk
flour
beaten egg

Sauce:
pork lard for frying
2 onions (200 g.), finely
  chopped
2 garlic cloves, minced
1 T. flour
3 *choricero* peppers (red
  peppers), boiled, with
  skins and seeds
  removed (save the
  water)
salt

To prepare the stuffing, fry the chopped onion and garlic in pork lard. Season the ground meat with salt, pepper, and white wine. When the onion and garlic mixture is tender, add the seasoned meat, stir, and remove from heat to cool for a short while. Add the bread crumbs, whole egg, and egg yolks and mix thoroughly.

Dry the large red peppers with a cloth and stuff with the meat mixture. Close at top with toothpicks. Roll the stuffed peppers in flour and beaten egg, then brown in pork lard. Remove the toothpicks and place the peppers in a separate pot.

Sauce

Using the remaining pork lard, fry the two chopped onions together with the minced garlic cloves. When the onion is slightly done, add one tablespoon of flour. When the mixture takes on a golden color, add the pulp of the previously boiled *choricero* peppers and cook for a short time. Then add some salt and the water in which the *choricero* peppers have been boiled. Pass this mixture through a food mill or blender.

Pour the sauce over the stuffed peppers. Add enough water to cover the peppers and cook on top of the stove until tender—about 30 minutes. Salt to taste and serve.

Basque Chicken
Pollo a la vasca

This dish has become very popular throughout the world. To my understanding, this fondness is due to the ability of the restaurant owners in the French Basque zone to successfully provide their customers with authentic Basque dishes.

The recipe (*poulet à la basquaise* in French) has changed significantly, in that the chickens used today are much younger than those that were used a few years ago. Now, chickens are given commercial feed instead of corn or other types of grain. The somewhat insipid taste of chicken meat is better masked in this dish than in roasted or baked preparations. Chicken is typically a tender meat, and if we know how to season it, we can make it quite agreeable to those people who still recall corn-fed, four-month-old chickens.

René Cuzacq (in my opinion the best Basque culinary writer on the other [French] side of the Pyrenees) provides three recipes for this dish, out of which I have selected the one provided to the master by Madame Poupel de Cambo.

⅔ cup (150 g.) olive oil
or pork lard
3⅓ lbs. (1500 g.) chicken
salt
pepper
minced garlic, to taste
1 medium onion (100 g.),
chopped
2 medium tomatoes (500
g.), cleaned and seeded

6 medium red peppers
(canned or fresh
roasted), peeled and
sliced
⅓ lb. (150 g.) ham, cut in
cubes
1 cup regional white
wine
½ lb. (200 g.)
mushrooms, cleaned
and sliced
Italian parsley, chopped

In a casserole dish, heat the olive oil or lard. Cut chicken into parts
and season with salt, pepper, and minced garlic. Place the chicken in the
pot and add the chopped onion, tomatoes, red peppers, and cubed ham.
Then add the wine and sliced mushrooms and cook over low heat for 30
minutes until tender. When the sauce is cooked down, add the chopped
parsley. Four servings.

This dish may be served on a platter surrounded by white rice,
which will soak up the sauce.

Small Wild Birds
Chimbos

In Basque gastronomy, *chimbos* is the name given to various species of small birds which in autumn are fattened up by plentiful foodstuffs available in the Basque mountains.

No human action intervenes in their feeding, and although these birds may have been abundant long ago, they are now scarce. Their gustatory qualities, however, excel those of the ortolan (European bunting) of Gascon cuisine.

According to Emiliano de Arriaga in his book *Lexicón Bilbaíno,* there are several varieties of these birds:

- black-tailed *chimbo*

- red-tailed *chimbo*

- black-headed or corn *chimbo*

- bramble *chimbo*

- fig tree *chimbo*

- royal *chimbo*

- anthill or wryneck *chimbo*

- whistling or grapevine *chimbo*

For many, the fig tree *chimbo* is the tastiest, given that its eating of that firm, rich fruit results in a singularly appetizing taste and aroma.

The recipe given here comes to us from the restaurant El Amparo and was published in *El Amparo: sus platos clásicos*, a book on its cuisine. I consider this work, written by Ursula Azcaray Eguileor et. al , one of the best written sources about Vizcayan Basque cooking.

2 chimbos (per serving)	**Italian parsley, chopped**
pork lard	**garlic clove, minced**
bread crumbs	**salt to taste**

Thoroughly clean and disembowel the birds. Remove the feet and beaks. Salt each *chimbu,* inside and out, and fry whole in the lard until done. The fat used in this recipe for frying these birds must be pork lard, although the *chimbos* possess a lot of fat which can be used along with the lard. Separate the fat from the birds during the cleaning process and add to the pork lard before frying the *chimbos.*

Remove the birds from the pan and set aside. Cover and keep warm. In the lard, place bread crumbs and a little chopped parsley and garlic. Stir this while heating. Cover each bird with the mixture, discarding some of the grease if necessary. (The bread crumb mixture can be made in the pan with the birds, if you wish.) Serve the *chimbos* in a little "nest" made of linen folded at the corners.

Although *El Amparo* does not specify quantities, a pair of *chimbos* constitutes one serving, according to our calculations.

Dove Ragout
Salmis de palomas

This autumn dish is typically prepared during the season when the doves pass over our country, fleeing the impending cold in search of the temperate southern zones. The French town of Sare is especially famous for this preparation.

If the doves are eaten by their captors, then my advice as to selection of the birds is not useful. However, for those who purchase the doves, I would advise that a young female has much more tender meat than that of an older male and is therefore more desirable. If the doves are tender, the preparation will be cooked in only half an hour.

Prior to making this dish, the doves are plucked and cleaned and left to set for a few days (hung upside down). A standard portion is half a dove per person.

2 doves
⅓ cup (100 g.) olive oil
¼ lb. (100 g.) bacon
½ lb. (200 g.) chopped mushrooms, preferably *onto-beltzak* (a *Boletus* species)
2 medium onions (200 g.) chopped
4 garlic cloves, minced
a little flour

4 T. tomato purée
4 cups meat broth or bouillon
4 cups good Rioja wine
⅓–½ cup (100 g.) grated carrot
4 sprigs aromatic herbs (rosemary, thyme, etc.)
various spices to taste
Armagnac (a dry brandy) for flaming

Select a skillet into which the pieces of dove will fit easily. Pour the olive oil into the skillet and add the bacon, mushrooms, onions, and garlic. When the chopped onions take on a golden color as a result of the action of the heat, add a little flour, then add the tomato purée, broth, wine, grated carrots, herbs, and spices. Simmer this mixture over low heat for 30 minutes.

Meanwhile, braise or lightly roast the doves until the juice from the breast runs pink. The best method of doing this is by placing them in a clay roaster and cooking for 20 minutes at 300° F (140° C).

Cut the cooked doves into quarters and reserve all the bones and pieces that will not be served in the final dish. Place these extra parts in the skillet with the sauce and cook slowly for another 15 minutes.

Place the quarters of dove in a hot serving dish. Remove the bones and extra dove parts from the skillet and pour the sauce over the main dish. Four servings.

This recipe is normally flamed. In the northern part of the Basque Country (where the best *salmis* of dove is served), the flaming is done with Armagnac. There are some cooks who put the doves to flame before adding the sauce, and others do it afterward. This dish is served very hot, and it proves to be a superb preparation.

DESSERTS

Rice Pudding
Arroz con leche

4 cups (1 liter) milk
1 whole cinnamon stick
⅓ cup (75 g., 2½ oz.)
short-grained rice,
rinsed thoroughly

½ cup (125 g., 4⅓ oz.)
sugar
ground cinnamon

Put milk on to cook with a stick of cinnamon. When it reaches a boil, remove the cinnamon stick and add the rinsed rice. Stir with a spatula, allowing the mixture to cook slowly over low heat. After 30 minutes, add the sugar and continue to cook for another 30 minutes. The mixture should result in a fine cream with loose grains of rice. Transfer to a serving bowl and sprinkle with ground cinnamon. Serve at room temperature or chilled. Four to six servings.

Rice Pudding Custard
Flan de arroz con leche

caramelized sugar for
coating mold
ingredients for *arroz
con leche* (see recipe
for rice pudding)
4 egg yolks, well beaten

about ½ cup chopped
fruit, such as currants,
raisins, etc., to taste
cream (optional)

Prepare rice pudding (see previous recipe). After the rice is cooked (the full 60 minutes), add the egg yolks and chopped fruit and stir quickly.

Caramelize sugar in a pan. Pour into a flan or custard mold and rotate quickly so that the caramel is distributed evenly and completely. Pour the pudding mixture into the mold and then place it in a pan containing about one inch of hot water (a *bain-marie* or *baño María* is used in Europe). Place pan on top of the stove over low heat (or in a low oven). To test for doneness, insert a toothpick in the middle. If done, the toothpick will come out dry. Chill in refrigerator. Loosen from mold, invert onto a platter, and serve alone or covered with cream. Four to six servings.

Rice Pudding Pastries
Pastelitos de arroz con leche

3 cups (850 g.) milk	bread crumbs
cinnamon or lemon peel (a little of one or the other)	beaten egg
	oil for frying
	sugar for dusting
⅓ cup (85 g.) rice	
½ cup (125 g.) sugar	

Add the cinnamon or lemon peel to the milk and bring to a boil. Add the rice and ½ cup of sugar. Cook slowly for 30 minutes. Cool the mixture, then scoop out by the spoonful and roll in bread crumbs like croquettes. Dip into beaten egg and roll again in bread crumbs. Fry in very hot oil, remove, and dust with sugar. The pastries should be served while hot.

Fried Custard Squares
Crema frita

4 egg yolks	1 T. butter, softened
⅓ cup (100 g.) sugar	flour
¼ cup (50 g.) flour	beaten egg
2 cups (½ liter) milk	oil and butter for frying
cinnamon	powdered or fine
	granulated sugar

Beat the egg yolks and add sugar and flour a little at a time, beating with a spatula until smooth. Add cinnamon to the milk and bring to a boil. Add the milk to the egg mixture while beating. Place the mixture in a saucepan with the tablespoon of butter; cook over medium heat while stirring continuously until it thickens (about 10 minutes).

Cool slightly and then pour into a square flat-bottomed pan greased with butter. Spread evenly and thinly (about ¼ inch) and chill in refrigerator for several hours. (Traditionally the pan was cooled by surrounding it with cold water.)

Remove from refrigerator and cut into small squares. Dip lightly into flour and beaten egg, then fry quickly in hot oil and butter (about 40 seconds on each side). Drain and sprinkle with powdered or fine granulated sugar and serve.

Custard
Flan

3 cups (12 *jícaras*) milk
18 cubes (6 T.) sugar
1 cinnamon stick

lemon or orange peel to
  taste
6 egg yolks
caramelized sugar

Mix milk, sugar cubes, cinnamon, and lemon or orange peel together and cook until quantity is reduced in half. Beat the egg yolks and add to the milk. Blend well and then strain the mixture.

Prepare a mold with caramelized sugar and pour the egg-milk mixture into it. Place the mold in a pan containing about one inch of hot water. Cook over low heat for a while and then place in the oven to brown the top. (Or bake in moderate oven, 325°–350° F). The custard will be done when a knife inserted in the center comes out clean. Cool in refrigerator. Loosen the cold custard from the mold and carefully invert onto a platter (caramel will drip). Four to six servings.

NOTE: A *jícara* is a small cup used for drinking chocolate. It is approximately the size of a demitasse cup, about 2 ounces.

Chestnut Custard
Flan de castañas

**2 lbs. (1 kilo) chestnuts,
roasted and peeled
2 cups (½ liter)
sweetened condensed
milk**

**4 egg whites
some vanilla for flavoring
caramelized sugar
whipped cream flavored
with vanilla**

Mash the chestnuts until a paste is formed. Add the milk, egg whites, and a little vanilla. Coat a mold with caramelized sugar and pour the chestnut mixture into the mold. Place the mold in a pan containing about one inch of hot water. Bake in a moderate oven until the mixture sets (test with toothpick).

Chill in refrigerator. Loosen from mold and invert onto a platter. Serve with the flavored whipped cream.

Rich Caramel Custard
Tocino de cielo ("Fat from Heaven")

**1 cup (250 g.) sugar
1½ cups water
grated lemon peel or
vanilla, according to
taste**

**7 egg yolks
1 whole egg**

Combine sugar, one cup of the water, and the lemon peel or vanilla and bring to a boil. Add the remaining water and continue boiling until this syrup mixture reaches a "fine thread" stage. Coat a custard mold with some of the above syrup.

Combine the egg yolks and whole egg in a bowl and beat well. Add the remaining syrup mixture, blend well, and run through a strainer. Pour into the syrup-coated mold and place in a *baño María* or pan containing about one inch of hot water. Cook slowly for ten minutes, then remove from water. Cover mold with linen paper or aluminum foil and place in a moderate oven (350° F) for about 13 minutes. Check periodically with a toothpick to make sure the egg yolk does not harden too much. Refrigerate until ready to serve. This dessert may also be made in individual dessert cups first coated with the syrup.

Soft Custard
Natillas

1½ cups (6 *jícaras*) milk	4 egg yolks
12 cubes (¼ cup) sugar	meringue (optional)
vanilla, cinnamon, or	
grated lemon peel	

Mix milk, sugar, and vanilla, cinnamon, or lemon peel together. Cook down until the mixture is reduced to one cup (4 *jícaras*). Remove from heat. Beat egg yolks until blended evenly, then add the milk mixture to the yolks.

Cook over very low heat (or in a double boiler), stirring gently until foam disappears (or until custard coats spoon with a thick, smooth layer when dipped into it). Remove from heat and run through a strainer into dessert bowl or custard cups. Cool and serve at room temperature with cookies or sponge cake, or garnish with spoonfuls of your own meringue for a floating island pudding. Two to four servings.

Basque Cake
Pastel vasco

1½ cups (250 g.) flour, sifted
½ cup (125 g.) sugar
a pinch of salt
½ cup (1 stick, 125 g.) butter, softened to room temperature
2 egg yolks

1 tsp. baking powder
1 lemon peel, grated
pastry cream for filling (sample recipe follows) flavored with rum or black cherry preserves
beaten egg

Put the flour in a large bowl. Make a hole in the middle and place in it the sugar, salt, butter, egg yolks, baking powder, and lemon peel. Work everything together very well into a dough.

Divide the dough into two balls and roll out flat into a crust with a rolling pin. Place one crust in a greased and floured 8-inch or 9-inch springform pan, shaping the dough against the sides. Fill the center with a very thick pastry cream, flavored with a little rum or some black cherry preserves. (Be sure that the filling does not touch the rim of the pan.) Cover with the other dough crust. Brush the top with beaten egg and scratch a harlequin (diamond) pattern on it with a fork. Bake for 25–30 minutes in an oven preheated to hot (400° F) and then turned down after 10 minutes to low (about 325° F). Alternate method: bake in a moderate oven—350° F—for 35 minutes. Four servings. Recipe from the French Basque provinces.

Pastry cream

This basic recipe for cream filling may be used for Basque cake, or another one may be selected by the cook.

¾ cup sugar
5–6 egg yolks
⅓ cup flour, sifted
pinch of salt
2 cups milk

1 tsp vanilla extract
flavorings (e.g., dark
  rum, black cherry
  preserves, almond
  extract) to taste

Mix sugar and egg yolks together until creamy and light colored. Add flour and salt; mix just enough to combine, but don't work it up. Add vanilla to milk and scald. Then add the milk little by little to the egg yolk mixture. Stir well to combine. Pour it back into the milk pan and cook, stirring vigorously until it reaches the boiling point. Boil for about two minutes, then remove from heat. Add flavoring of your own choice and stir in. Strain and let cool. Stir or strain occasionally to prevent a crust from forming.

Sweet Fried Bread
Torrijas

1 loaf day-old French
  bread
1 pint (½ liter) milk
3 T. sugar
1 cinnamon stick

2 or 3 eggs, beaten well
oil or butter for frying
powdered sugar
ground cinnamon

Cut the bread loaf into small slices about 3/4 inch (2 centimeters) thick. Combine milk with sugar and the cinnamon stick, bring to a boil, and then chill. Add some of the cold milk to a wide bowl and soak the slices of bread in it for about five minutes. Turn the bread over, add the remaining milk, and leave for an hour to fully soak up the milk. (Then remove the slices to a dry dish and leave for at least an hour to dry.)

Heat oil or butter in a frying pan. Dip the slices of bread in beaten egg. Remove with a spoon or spatula having many holes so that the bread will drain without falling apart. Place the bread in the frying pan and fry until golden, carefully turning once. Drain well. Roll the bread pieces in powdered sugar and then sprinkle with ground cinnamon. These *torrijas* may be served hot or cold, although it is better to serve them hot. Four servings.

Bibliography

THERE are other fine sources of information about food and cooking in the Basque Country. A few volumes mention Basque cuisine only in passing. Many of them are old and probably difficult to obtain. All of them are in European languages. The author has provided a list of these books in appreciation of what they have contributed to this volume.

Aranzadi Unamuno, Telesforo. *Setas u hongos del País Vasco. Guía para la distinción de los comestibles y venenosos. (Euskalerrico perrechikuak.)* Madrid: Romo y Füssel, 1897.

Arias de Apraiz, Elvira. *Libro de cocina o pequeña recopilación de recetas culinarias por Elvira de Apraiz (una Vitoriana).* 40th printing. Vitoria: Vda. e Hijos de Sra, 1953.

Arocena Arregui, Fausto. *El País Vasco visto desde fuera.* Biblioteca Vascongada de los Amigos del País, Monografías Vascongadas, no. 1. San Sebastián (Zarauz): Icharopena, 1949.

Arraiza, Francisco Javier. *La cocina navarra. Recetario de platos navarros. Nomenclatura euskérica de los principales utensilios de la cocina navarra.* Pamplona: Bengaray, 1930.

Arriaga Ribero, Emiliano de. *Lexicón bilbaíno.* Biblioteca Vasca VI. 2nd edition. Madrid: Minotauro, 1960.

Azcaray Eguileor, Ursula y Sira. *El Amparo: sus platos clásicos. Explicados por las mismas cocineras de aquella famosa cocina bilbaína, las hijas de doña Felipa Eguileor, señorita Ursula y Sira . . .* 4th printing. Bilbao: Escuelas Gráficas de la Santa Casa de Misericordia, 1949.

Bardají, Teodoro. *La cocina de ellas.* Madrid: 1955.

Beleak, Imanol [Manuel Cuervas-Mons, pseud.]. *El libro del pescado. Las mejores recetas de cocina vasca; id. internacional y un apéndice.* San Sebastián: Itxaropena, 1933.

Buesa, Andres. *Las setas. Descripción y láminas, señalando con seguridad las setas comestibles.* Vitoria: Imprenta Provincial, 1950.

Calera, Ana María. *La cocina vasca.* Bilbao: Editorial La Gran Enciclopedia Vasca, 1976.

Camba, Julio. *La casa de Lúculo; o, El arte de comer (nueva fisiología del gusto).* Madrid: Compañía iberoamericana de publicaciones, 1929.

D. V. de U. Bilbao: Imprenta de El Noticiero Bilbaino, 1903.

Domenech, Ignacio. *La cocina vasca (Laurak Bat).* Barcelona: Publicaciones Selectas de Cocina, 1935.

Entrambasaguas Peña, Joaquín de. *Loa de los vinos de Rioja.* Logroño: Cámara de Comercio de Logroño, n.d.

Escualdun cocinera ceinarekin nornabic cocina ona errechki eguin baitaçake. Bayonne: Cluzeau, 1864.

García de Salazar, Lope. *Las bienandanzas e fortunas.* Códice del siglo xv. Facsímil. Bilbao: A. Rodríguez Herrero, 1955.

Ibarguren, Félix. Recipes published in *El Pueblo Vasco* newspaper, San Sebastián.

Irigoyen, Juan. Recipes published in *La Gaceta de Norte* newspaper, Bilbao.

Juaristi, Adriana de. *Cocina.* Madrid: Espasa-Calpe, 1932.

Lezama, Mercedes. *Mi cocina vizcaina económica.* Bilbao, n.d.

Mendizabal, López. *Cocinan icasteco liburua.* Tolosa, 1889.

Mestayer de Echagüe, María [Marquesa de Parabere, pseud.]. *Enciclopedia culinaria.* Madrid: Espasa-Calpe, n.d.

Palay, Simon. *La cuisine du pays: Armagnac, Béarn, Bigorre, Landes, Pays Basque. 500 recettes de cuisine, pâtisserie, confiserie.* Pau: Marrimpouey, 1951.

Pomiane, Eduard de. *La physique de la cuisine.* Paris: Editions Albin Michel, n.d.

Pradera, Nicolasa. *La cocina de Nicolasa.* 7th printing. Madrid: Ribadeneyra, 1950.

Saiz y Saldain, Luís. *Inspección Bromatológica.* San Sebastián: Martín, Mena y ca., 1913.

Ruíz Zabalza, Genoveva. *Geno y su cocina.* Pamplona: Gómez, 1952.

Virgen del Carmen, Fr. G. de la. *Apuntes de cocina para uso de los hermanos carmelitas descalzos.* Vitoria: Domingo Star, 1922.

Index

chestnut: consumption of, 10–11, 115; flour from, 18; nutritional value of, 11; recipe for, **186**; roasting of, 8, 115

chicken, 52, 168; quality of, 176; recipes for, 63, **176–77**

chicory, 43

chilindrón, 62, 63, **168–69**

chimbos, 63, **178–79**; types of, 178

chipirones. See squid

chives, 44

chocolate, 18, 19, 116

chops: of Azpeitia, 55–58, 59; Bilbao style, 60; consumption of, 57; lamb, 59, 62; pork, 62; preparation method for, 55, 56–57; serving of, 57, 58

choricero. See pepper, *choricero*

chorizo, Basque, 63–64, 114; as ingredient, 45, 47, 62, 128; types of, 64

Christmas, foods eaten at, 37, 40, 75, 92, 130

cider: as beverage, 86, 120–21, 153; in historical diet of Basques, 10, 12, 17, 22; as recipe ingredient, 79, 84, 107, 120

Cinco Villas Aragonesas, wheat from, 30

cinnamon, 44; as recipe ingredient, 115, 116, 117, 182, 183, 184, 185, 190

clams, 77, 105, 108

climate: effect of, 36–37, 114–15; of Basque Country, 21; for rice cultivation, 31

clove, 44, 68

cocido (Basque boiled dinner), 15, 20, 34, 107; of Labourd, 46; preparation of, 45–46, 47

cod, 12, 17, 97–102; curing of, 98; desalting of, 99, 100, 135, 154, 156; economic importance of, 98; ingredient of *porrusalda,* 39, 45, **135**; preliminary preparation of, 99–102; quality of, 98, 100; recipe for, 41, 44, 45, 99, 101–2, **135**, **154–55**, **156–57**; tempering of, 100

cod fishing, 3, 98; beginning of, by Basques, 12; decline of, 18

cognac, 81, 148, 149, 162, 163, 168, 169

comber, 92

confit d'oie, 63, 64

cooking methods: for meat, 52–64; primitive, 5–7, 30–31

Corella, 44

corn: as animal feed, 15, 113; as dependable crop, 14; grown with beans, 15; hybridization of, 29–30; introduction of, 13–14; meal, 28–29; rotation with wheat and turnips, 15; spoilage of flour, 29

corvina, 92

court-bouillon, 106

cousinette a la Bayonnaise, 46

crab: preparation of, 41; spider, 41, 80–81, **161**, **162–63**; types of, 78, 80

tato), 45, **134–35**; octopus, 71; seasonings in, 44. *See also marmitako; tioro*

stewed dishes, 61–63

stewing, of meat, procedures for, 60–61

Strabo, 9, 10

strawberries, 115

sweetbreads, 61, 62

sweets, 116–18

talo, 12, 28–29, 33

taloburni, 8, 28

tamboliña (tamboril), 8, 115

tarragon, 44, 114

ternasco, 51

thyme, 44, 66, 145

tioro, preparation of, 41, 107, **142–43**

tocino de cielo, 117, **186–87**

Tolosa: beans of, 15; recipes of, 61, 116, **170–71**

tomatoes, 41, 90, 95, 99, 114; cultivation of, 41; in *menestra,* 46

tongue: calves', 61; dried, 64; Tolosan, 61, **170–71**

torrijas, **190**

tortas, 12

tortilla española, 141

toxin: fish, 90, 96, 97; squid ink, 73

transportation, of agricultural products, 22, 119, 123

Treviño, 51, 169

tripe, 62, 66

tripoches, 6

trout, 83–84, **160**

truffle, 26–27, 73

Tudela, 116, 132

tuna, 95, 108, 109, **144–45**; **146–47**; cured, 19. *See also marmitako*

turbot, 97, **158**

turnip, 15; as forage, 35

turtles: eggs of, 112; sea, 68

txakolin. See chacolí

txangurro, preparation of, 41, 80–81, **161**, **162–63**

Urbasa, cheese of, 57, 119

Urbía, cheese of, 57, 119

Urola River, 55–56

Usua Busca, doña, 174

utensils, 68, 124, 146, 159, 183; iron, 8; for meats, 54, 55; primitive, 4, 7–8

Valencia, *paella* of, 20, 31

Van Eys, Mathilde, 19

Van Eys, Willem J., 19

veal, consumption of, 50, 170, 172

vegetables: aversion of Basque farmers and peasants to, 9; preparation methods for, 44–47

Vergara, 116, 117

vetch, blue, 32

vinegar, 114

Virgen del Carmen, Fr. G. de la, 136

Virgen del Carmen (holy day), 85

Vitoria, 17, 51, 79, 116, 131, 136

Vizcaya: beverage of, 121; blood sausages of, 66; fish consumed in, 87; foods historically consumed in, 17; potato consumption in, 35

Vizcayan-style (*a la vizcaina*): recipes, 43, 62, 86, 100–101, 179; sauce, 44, 101, 106, **146**, **147**

walnuts, 61, 115
weevers, 97
whale: consumption of, 13, 51; hunting of, 13, 18, 98
wheat, 12; flour, 30; planted with beans, 33; quality of, 30; rotation with corn and turnips, 15; scarcity of, 17, 18; shipment of, 22
whiting, 98
wildfowl, quality of, 52

wine: of Belloc, 120; consumption of, 18, 19, 99; of Irouleguy, 63, 120; Navarrese, 22, 120; Rioja, 57, 119–20, 136, 180; of Saint-Étienne-de-Baigorry, 120; white, as recipe ingredient, 46, 68, 80, 107, 114, 115, 121, 133, 170. *See also chacolí*
woodcock, 52
wrasses, 94
wreckfish, 91

Zaldivia, consumption of sausages in, 6–7
Zarauz, 120, 138
zato, 8
zezina, 64
Zumaya, 77
zurrakapote, 115
zurrukutuna, 99

DESIGN BY DAVE COMSTOCK

EDITORIAL SUPERVISION BY CAMERON SUTHERLAND

COMPOSITION BY G&S TYPESETTERS, AUSTIN, TEXAS

PRINTING AND BINDING BY THOMSON-SHORE, INC., DEXTER, MICHIGAN

About the author

The late José María Busca Isusi, a leading Basque gastronomer, lived in Zumárraga in the Basque province of Guipúzcoa, Spain. He specialized in creating tasty and attractive meals that were affordable for almost all Basques. His *arroz blanco con mejillones* (white rice with mussels) is an example of an inexpensive meal that can compete with costly recipes—it won the regional gastronomy contest in Guipúzcoa in 1967. Busca Isusi had a regular column in the San Sebastián newspaper *Diario Vasco* and wrote several books on gastronomy, including *Guía gastronomica de Guipúzcoa* (*Gastronomic Guide of Guipúzcoa*), *Guía para recolectar las principales setas comestibles* (*Guide to the Gathering of the Principal Edible Mushrooms*), and *La cocina vasca del pescado y marisco* (*Basque Cooking for Fish and Seafood*).